Managing with Appraisal

David Trethowan has vast experience of leading practical courses in aspects of management in schools, as well as contributing regularly to the courses of major international companies such as IBM and Barclays Bank. He writes specialist school management handbooks for the Industrial Society, and is a leading national authority on teaching appraisal. He has 25 years experience in the profession, 15 of them as a head of a very successful comprehensive school. He is now an independent consultant to a small number of LEAs in England, Scotland and Wales.

Managing with Appraisal

Achieving Quality Schools through Performance Management

David M. Trethowan

P·C·P
Paul Chapman
Publishing Ltd

Paul Chapman Publishing Ltd
144 Liverpool Road
London
N1 1LA

British Library Cataloguing in Publication Data
Trethowan, David
    Managing with appraisal: achieving quality schools
    through performance management.
    1. Schools. Teachers. Assessment
    I. Title
    371.144

    ISBN 1–85396–135–3

Typeset by Inforum Typesetting, Portsmouth
Printed by St Edmundsbury Press, Bury St Edmunds
Bound by W.H. Ware, Clevedon, Avon

CONTENTS

INTRODUCTION

Performance management has four distinct facets:

- Culture creation and goal-setting (and managing changes in them).
- Staff development (including training and planned experience).
- Appropriate management (including styles, skills and practices).
- Appraisal of performance (including the appraising relationship and the interview).

Now, it would be attractive to be able to view these facets as operating consecutively. First the climate is set, then the goals, followed by staff training and development leading to appropriate management and, finally, the appraisal of performance. Just as attractive is the cycle which runs as shown in Figure 1. Sometimes this relationship holds true and the performance is managed in that sequence. But more frequently, in practice, a variety of sequences is followed, for example where a planned experience for teacher development results from appraisal, from the ongoing process of management or from the initial setting of goals. Equally often, goals are set following a developmental experience or at the end of an appraisal. In short, there is no fixed sequence in which the four key elements operate within the performance management cycle. But operate they clearly do.

A further feature of the four facets of performance appraisal, in a healthy management relationship, is that the sequence seldom applies simultaneously to all the tasks which a teacher is performing.

At any one time, in one aspect of the teacher's work it may be appropriate to set goals, in another to be undertaking development, in a third aspect to participate in management decision-making and in a fourth to be making

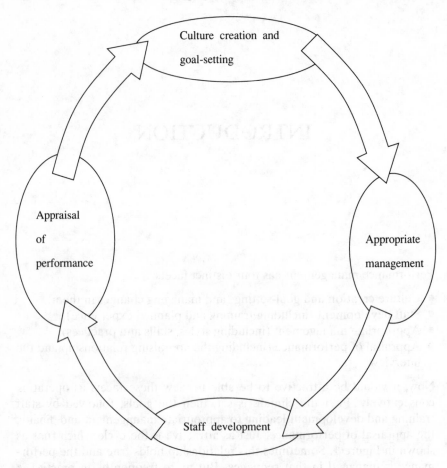

Figure 1 Performance management.

an appraisal of a completed activity. Nevertheless, within the context of every effective management situation these four features combine to create performance management. Performance management is an ongoing, continuous process and its four inter-relating facets are, in this book, known as the 'appraising relationship'. Schools which successfully develop appraising relationships within them are herein called 'appraising schools'.

Performance management is essential to all schools, whether those schools are primary or secondary, whether they have opted for grant-maintained status or remained under a more traditional management. It matters not whether there is a National Curriculum, open enrolment or local management of schools (LMS). Unless teacher performance is managed successfully, no school will achieve its potential. Financial management, resource management, curriculum management and every other form of management all have their role, but they pale into insignificance beside the effective management of teacher performance. If those who lead schools cannot develop the skills of managing people, an underachieving school will inevitably result from their efforts.

The Education (No. 2) Act of 1986 lays out the parameters within which education in the 1990's is required to devleop in England and Wales. Likewise, the 1991 Regulations set the framework for the development of school teacher appraisal. But neither those Education Act Regulations nor the accompanying circular to Local Education Authorities can legislate for the relationship which makes performance management or any of its four component parts, work. Clear as the regulations are about who appraises, about the collection of information, about the form and the frequency of appraisal interviews and about the writing and retention of appraisal statements – nothing in such a Statutory instrument can create an appraising relationship. And appraisal is only effective within the appraising relationship which we are about to examine. In the appraising school, within the appraising relationship, those who manage and appraise the performance of others make the most of critical opportunities to improve their teachers' performances through specific management practices. It is that relationship and those specific practices which are described in this book.

One final point should be drawn to the reader's attention. This book has been written as a companion to an earlier volume in this series, *Appraisal and Target Setting: A Handbook for Teacher Development* (Trethowan, 1987). Though both books are intended as complete works in themselves, certain aspects which are developed fully in one book have not had that development repeated in the other. For those seeking a full and complete account of the integration of appraisal and performance management, the books should be read as one.

PART I
CULTURE CREATION AND GOAL-SETTING

1
THE VISION

The first essential for the successful school is that you, its leader, have a vision of the school as it will be at its best. I do not mean that you have occasional flashes of inspiration about the establishment, but rather that you live with that vision, day by day and hour by hour. There must be absolute clarity in the leader's mind about what constitute the key features of this vision. The vision has to be hard, well thought out and practical. The leader has to believe in it, for he or she gets fire and inspiration from it. This is the vision the leader will use as a touchstone to make decisions, to prioritize, to test success and to raise the morale of staff when it is low. For most leaders I believe the stirrings of a vision are within them well before they reach the leadership position. You know what excellence is in the abstract, but what would this particular school be doing if it were an excellent one? Your vision has to be related to time and place. No good school has ever been created without such a vision, and no school continues to be good once the vision of those who lead it has been lost.

The importance of vision can be illustrated from the experience of a client for whom I carried out consultancy work. He was the headmaster of the grammar school of a thriving market town from 1954 to 1974, and thereafter head of the comprehensive school which it became. He said to me:

'You talk about vision. I came to this school with such a vision of a school with the highest standards of conduct, academic attainment and sporting achievement. I drew a staff around me who believed in that vision as much as I did and within a few years we had made that dream a virtual reality. The vision was communicated to the town through our performance. We were respected, appreciated and understood by the whole community. When, in the early '70s, they began to make us a comprehensive school I tried to create a vision of the new school, but I couldn't. It did not fit either with my beliefs or with those of my longstanding colleagues. We went through the motions of organization and rhetoric but what developed was a shadow of the former school. I gave it all I could for four years, but my retirement was a happy release. My successor believed wholeheartedly in such schools and except for a few departures convinced the staff of its value and purpose. To be quite fair, I would say it is about as good a school recently as it was 20 years ago, but in a very different way. I tell you this to support what you were saying about the need for the head to have a mental image, an objectification, of the school which is being developed.

Features of an organizational vision

The features of an organizational vision are:

1. Your vision must be related to a specific school in a specific time period. My vision for a comprehensive school in suburban Hayward's Heath in the 1970s was vastly different from the vision for the comprehensive in which I had previously worked on the edge of urban Shepherd's Bush in the late 1960s.
2. Your vision has been selected from all the other possible visions of the school as the option which comes closest to meeting the needs of its customers. By customers I mean those people who make the decision whether or not to send a child to your school – the parents. Customer needs are most often expressed as
    – the quality of education their children are to receive and
    – being able to conduct a constructive dialogue with the school about that education.
3. Your vision has your obvious, wholehearted commitment . Exhibit that commitment by being highly visible in the school, by taking and support-ing action towards the achievement of the vision. Reinforce that com-mitment by walking around the school while it is in session every day; sending a memorandum to staff from behind a closed office door has nothing like the same impact.
4. Your vision is so attractive that it motivates staff to work towards it. It has to become their vision, too. Since you want to attract others to it, make sure the vision will achieve something positive for education and is not merely organizational megalomania. Your aim is that the staff are proud to work towards the vision and would be proud to work in the school when the vision is achieved.
5. Your vision expects to be both developed and evaluated over time as needs or resources change. It knows there are no organizational visions which have the right to be permanent.

Sources of the vision

The three groups of factors which contribute to the building of a vision are:

1. Factors within the leader – his or her own beliefs and values.
   The head needs to be as aware as possible of what he or she believes to be of value in education. That invigorating managerial purpose you can call your own, will be your driving force long after your school is operating at a reasonable level and you are tempted to let it rest there. Inner belief will keep you looking for new ways to improve.
2. Factors in the school – its history, clientele, staff, resources and potential.
3. Factors in the milieu – society's expectations of education and the purposes that society requires education to serve.

In my own case, when leading a school in the early 1970s, society seemed to want individualized education within comprehensive schools. Local parents, when I took up the post, said they wanted 'good discipline and good results' for their children, and later they added 'good teaching' and 'strong encouragement to develop as happy and confident young people'. The residual staff seemed to think that the school had fallen below its earlier high, secondary modern standards and wanted very much to be part of developing a successful comprehensive school. For my own part the vision was rooted in my past. That led to a belief in, and an enthusiasm for, a school based on supportive relationships – giving each child a positive environment in which to develop. This meant more than removing the negatives – poor, dispirited or bigoted teaching and pupils with dwindling respect for themselves or for others. It meant developing the positives – a pride not only in one's own performance but in the performance of others in the school, namely other pupils, other teachers, other departments. It meant a particular form of school ethos, a pastoral care system which was not overloaded and only had time for social and emotional fire-fighting, but which actively sought out pupil problems. It meant an obvious commitment to pupil development, a sensitivity to the wishes of parents as the customers of the school, a school which consistently bettered last year's performance, a school which actively strove for excellence in all aspects of school life.

These and visions like them may seem millennialist and even unattainable, but they will be the long-term targets from which agreed, realistic short-term targets can be extrapolated. Be assured that such goals are not achieved by accident. They are achieved because someone had the vision of how a school could be and then had the technique, tenacity and tactical planning to turn that vision into a working reality.

What if you, as head, have no vision towards which the organization will strive? Then it is absolutely vital that you develop such a vision. If you cannot, the best alternative is to take the first opportunity to leave the post. But with the new interest, new influence and new expectation of society in its schools, identifying the vision is easier than it has been for 20 years. Times change and we change with them. Identifying a timely vision is a fundamental of educational leadership. And no one has greater responsibility for it than the leader.

Informing the vision

The vision is not a dream; dreams can exist in the mind of the dreamer and bear no relation to reality. A vision is an informed dream; it has been talked down to earth in discussions which relate it to time and place. Use any means at your disposal to inform the vision. Use consultants, surveys, questionnaires and interviews. But informing the vision essentially means questioning and listening to people, especially to those people who deliver what the school offers and to the customers who receive it.

The focus of the research to inform the vision is in three chief areas: the performance of the school, the attitudes within the school and the needs of its customers. This information is essential to create two views of the school:

- your assessment of the way it is at present and
- your vision of how it could be.

The space between these two views is the development gap. The plan for filling the gap will be the school strategic plan.

Create your own checklist for establishing present performance:

- How do you and others describe the organizational climate?
- What is the school's present purpose?
- How relevant is that purpose?
- How good is the school at achieving this?
- What are the chief difficulties under which staff work?
- What natural advantages does the school appear to have?
- What are its best features, its strengths and capabilities?
- What are its worst features?
- How does it compare with other schools nationally and locally?
- How does it shape up on some key performance indicators?
  - performance in external examinations at 16;
  - entry rates into continuing education at 16;

- participation in sporting, social, cultural activities;
- attendance, absenteeism and truancy rates;
- the manner and demeanour of the students;
- the attitude of staff.
- How is it seen by customers and by potential customers?
- What can the local primary heads tell you about your school?

A new head would be assembling this view of the school to take stock of the school he or she was about to lead. Heads in post are increasingly conducting a 'school review', which covers much of this ground, often encouraged and supported by the LEA (local education authority). By whatever means seems appropriate, it is vital to compile the truest possible snapshot of the school as it is. If you misunderstand where you are starting from, getting anywhere else from there will be that much harder.

Now apply this same information on present performance, attitudes and customer needs to visualizing what the school could be in the future. Ask yourself, 'What would an excellent school be achieving in this area, with these customers at this time?' Describe what you feel could be achieved by that excellent school. Make clear what the organization could be and how it could be seen. Check the vision against feedback from governors, staff, parents, LEA – anyone who has a valid perception of the school. This means face-to-face talking and listening. The vision becomes clearer as it is closely questioned, discussed and contested. When enough of this has been done the head will be in a position to describe the best possible school which the present organization could become. Describe this vision in writing and present it for the agreement of the governing body.

One way to present the vision is in the form of a mission statement. Dave Francis believes that the key features of a mission statement:

- state the strategic driving force of the organization (i.e. identify what the organization is devoted to doing well);
- say what the organization is not;
- are cautiously optimistic (realistic and believable);
- arise from deeds and personal beliefs, not wishful hopes;
- avoid high-sounding and pious wording;
- are lucid and readily understandable;
- show benefit to customers, teachers and governors;
- respect the distinguished history of the organization;
- include values towards pupils, parents, teachers, governors and communities;
- answer the question 'Why would we be proud to work for this school?'

Be willing to clarify, explain and defend. When governors agree, as they will, to a well-researched plan for an excellent school, publish it for all to see. This is the vision towards which the school will strive.

Putting the vision into practice

The next move is to analyse the gap between what exists at present and what the vision requires to happen in the future. Clarify possible strategies for closing the gap. High but achievable targets are the aim. Draw staff teams and their leaders into making a realistic five-year strategic plan. Consider the uncertainty in the national educational climate, the risks of change and of not changing, and the optimum use of resources. How to manage change is examined in detail later in this book (see pp. 13–20). In my experience five-year plans are revised every three years and only these first three early years need to be very detailed. It is from this strategic planning that departments and individuals will draw up their basic task in the school and will propose their targets. It is from this strategy that the school will plan its staff development and training, will identify its management techniques to enable teachers to maximize their achievement and will encourage the appraising relationship which feeds future performance.

When putting the vision into practice,

- show your enthusiasm;
- make commitments and keep them, even if they are a risk;
- be willing to restructure the school establishment to reflect its new purpose;
- put finance into the new fields of development;
- respect all your staff. In making the vision a reality it is better to pull people along with you than to push them where you want them to go;
- don't make false claims for progress towards the vision, because people close to the action will know it to be a hollow lie.

When success begins to show, trumpet it for all to hear. Praise the success and be proud of it. Make absolutely the most of it. It increases the self-esteem of the staff who helped in its achievement. And it will draw in many of those who at first stood aloof from the vision. People want to identify with success.

As a practical illustration of a new head bringing in a new vision for a school, I offer this personal recollection. As the newly appointed head of Warden Park School, in Sussex, I remember walking into my first staff meeting and announcing 'I am going to make this school the best school in the area. Help me if you want, but don't get in my way.' It would be difficult to recommend the particular style epitomized in that statement, but it was being made by someone without the benefit of management development, in a situation where uncertainty had prevailed, in an attempt to give us an aim, a purpose, a direction. The situation needed a strategic plan and a launch into action to allow the school to settle to its new structure and purpose. Accordingly, within a matter of weeks of joining the school I had interviewed every member of staff, produced a five-year plan and a new staffing establishment. Within a single term appointments had been made to every new and proposed post in the school. Almost every departmental head had been replaced and a pastoral care system had been installed where none had existed before, replacing a situation which relied heavily on the previous head and deputy recollecting the name and face of every pupil.

When I took up the headship in April 1973, in a document presented to the local education authority I wrote: 'The greatest need in this school is for a pastoral care system, for even at present it has grown too large to leave to chance the exercising of a caring concern for the whole child. At present senior staff are being greatly overstretched in an attempt to cover pastoral work satisfactorily.' I wanted both the pastoral structure and the new academic structure in operation within three months of my arrival, with 12 months of 'dry run' time to iron out any faults before we accepted our first comprehensive intake in September 1974. New heads of department were appointed to the art, English, history, languages, mathematics, music, boys' physical education, remedial, religious education and science departments. Of these new departmental heads, only four had previous experience as a head of department and the average age of the remainder was 27, with their average teaching experience on appointment being less than five years. The disadvantage of inexperience in this important field of departmental headship, I felt, could be offset by constant encouragement, support and guidance from me. This was the origin of an 'appraising relationship' and led to the rapid growth of an appraisal system at the school.

The vision in this case was put into place exceptionally quickly

- because of the need to remove the anxiety arising from longstanding uncertainty;
- because of the shortness of time before the school became comprehensive;
- because the lack of comprehensive school experience among the existing staff did not allow them to modify greatly the vision at that stage.

Full advantage was taken of a prevailing climate of change in education such as is even more strongly evident today. However, the secret of success in my view was not only in incorporating many staff ideas into the new policy and programmes, but in giving every possible member of the staff a development opportunity – a change of career direction, a responsibility, a promoted post, a delegated task. Each person had a stake in the success of the new school. Within a few years that school 'no longer depended on me but on a team of dedicated and confident staff, who through delegation and participation share in every aspect of management.' Within a few years it was true to say that 'all associated with the school perpetuate with pride the ethos of our school'.

Despite being inexpertly presented, the launch of the new school contained all the essential elements of translating a vision into high but achievable targets on which teams and individual teachers could begin work. Much had been done to change the organizational aspect of the school culture, but much more remained to be achieved in fields where change was far more difficult – the fields of values, beliefs and relationships.

2
ESTABLISHING THE CORPORATE CULTURE

The three elements of school culture

The most powerful factor in making the vision a reality is the personal identity of the school – its characteristic spirit or what industrial managers call its 'corporate culture'. Schein (1985) suggests that building the culture of an organization may be the most important task a leader has to achieve. This culture has three key components: ethos, organization and people (see Figure 2). Of these three aspects of culture, the simplest one to create, to identify or to change is the organization of a school. I do not wish to say that the organization of a school is simple nor that it is unimportant. In fact it is fundamental to successful working that, for example, teachers know to whom they are accountable, for what they are accountable and that they have the means of reliable, frank and frequent communication. Good heads set up such structures and work on organization and administration as being essential to maximizing teacher performance.

School organization is one of the chief factors comprising the conditions under which teachers work. It is far from unimportant. Ask any teacher who has worked in a school where the organizational aspect of culture is poor and that teacher will tell of frustration, wasted effort and conflict. Poor performance in one of the three areas which comprise school culture affects performance in the others. Poor school organization, therefore, affects both personal relationships and ethos, as is illustrated in Figure 2. But it is important to stress the need to identify, create or change the other

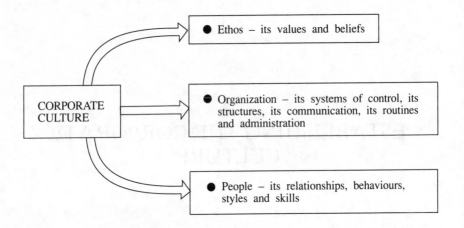

Figure 2   Corporate culture.

two facets of school culture – the ethos of the school and the performance of its people. Most of this book is devoted to the performance of people but it is essential to appreciate that the ethos of a school does not have to be subject to random forces but can be created, developed and managed.

Managing the ethos of a school

The ethos of a school may be defined as the set of values and beliefs which are shared by most members of the organization. These values are long term and not easy to change. They deeply influence a school because they are the touchstone by which people decide what is right, good and correct or bad, wrong and incorrect within an organization. The values are developed over time as people undertake an action in school and receive a message from those inside the organization about how that action is perceived. Those with influence in an organization are implicitly or explicitly telling others, 'This is the way we do things here'.

Every organization has this value-base or ethos. Its ethos is either planned and managed or it has developed under the influence of chance factors, serendipitous incidents and random personalities. Since that ethos will have such powerful influence on the attitude, behaviour and achievement of the school, it is essential that those who manage schools take care to manage the ethos. Any planned change within a school which does not take account of the existing ethos runs the risk of failure. A negative, destructive, anti-achievement ethos will continue to generate a poor school no matter what changes of staff, systems or structure are introduced. Faced with such a situation the head needs a strategy for dealing with the inappropriate ethos. Does the head

1. Disregard the ethos? If so, the head will be trying to introduce changes which are rejected by the existing values of the organization. Change will be doubly difficult to implement and may founder altogether.
2. Manage round the ethos, altering the strategy to minimize the conflict? This certainly has its merits if in large part the ethos is one in which the change can flourish and if the alterations to the strategy do not compromise the long-term vision of the school.
3. Change the ethos? This implies changing those parts of the ethos which would inhibit the implementation of the strategy. Select from the traditions of the past those values and beliefs which help or at least do not hinder the implementation of the change. Identify them, praise them as being part of the previous tradition that will be retained. In destroying what was previously valued by a school, even if those values were not very laudable, be careful not leave the school without perceived values. The value vacuum will be filled, perhaps with values that are even more inhibiting than the original ones.

When to opt for changing the ethos

When deciding whether the ethos of a school should be changed, the head should consider whether any of the following conditions apply. If they do, it is prudent to plan to change the ethos.

1. The school is certain to undergo major change in function and perhaps in size. This may apply in the future to some schools which become direct grant schools. It happened to many small schools with the advent of comprehensivization. Those schools which changed only their organization but failed to acknowledge and tackle the issue of an inappropriate ethos made scant success of the change, frequently bringing into disrepute the principle of comprehensive schooling.
2. The school is operating badly. It is considered an unsatisfactory establishment by its customers, its governors and possibly by its teachers. Rolls may be falling and reports from the national and local inspectorate confirm that performance is poor.
3. The school has an ethos which is out of tune with the environment in which it is operating or will have to operate. This is the case with many schools still finding it difficult to come to terms with the ramifications of the Education Reform Act 1988.

Minimizing resistance to changing the school ethos

Organizations and the people within them do not change their values and beliefs without a struggle. However, resistance to change can be minimized.

1. Make sure people are aware of the necessity for the change and the benefits which come from it. Never assume that promulgation of your view of the need for change means acceptance by those who fear they will have to suffer it. Remind people in many ways of what is required and how they will gain. 'What's in it for me?' is the question more likely to be implied than asked directly. But answer that question, none the less.
2. Allow people room to identify with the change. Indicate what has to be achieved but do not assume you have to tell people exactly how to do it. They are very likely to know best how to implement change in their own areas. Change is less threatening to people when they can feel they have some influence or control over it, and even less so if they can manage the change themselves.
3. Expect all those in management posts to display commitment to the change, especially top management. Show commitment in actions and attitudes as well as in words.
4. Be honest about which components of the change are open to negotiation and which are not. Never pretend to be participating and negotiating when you are really persuading, selling or telling. Staff will accept that some fundamental features of the plan are not open to negotiation; make this clear to them, explaining why they are so. But be sure to leave as much as possible, without jeopardizing success, for those involved to plan. If people prefer, from a lack of confidence or of willingness, to be told what to do, then happily adopt that style and move the change forwards.

How to set about changing the school ethos

1. *Make staff aware of the present ethos* and of why it is inappropriate as a basis for future development. From discussion with those who serve the school and those who are served by it, you need an analysis of the values and beliefs of the school. Draw up your analysis from listening to the answers to questions and from observing actions. Your analysis needs to uncover the organizational attitude towards working at the school and towards the education that is being provided. Consider such issues as:

- What is this school really aiming to produce?
- Are staff appropriately proud of their school?

- Who do staff believe are their customers?
- Is the school really trying to produce a first-class service?
- Is the school able to handle change?
- Do people want to improve the school?
- How do people in this organization relate to each other?

The collated answers to these questions will indicate where the ethos has to be changed or strengthened. Make staff aware of what you see as inappropriate values. Remember that people may have staked a large part of their working life upon some of the values you now seek to change. Even if you can convince such people in an academic debate of the need to adopt new values, it may not be easy for them to do so. They may be able to accept intellectually what they cannot act upon emotionally. Even so the second step is to lay out the new values.

2. *Publicize the new values* and encourage discussion of them by all who have influence over the delivery of education at the school – its governors and staff. Encourage discussion, too, of 'the way things are here'. Comparison between the new values and the old will help people to break into the cycle of new expectation and new achievement. In your role as head, present the new vision to the school and explain why the new values are necessary. Show your commitment and enthusiasm for them. Show the values in practice in all that you do. If your immediate colleagues in the senior management team have accepted the new values, encourage them to be good as ambassadors, perhaps with the advantage of having operated within the former ethos.

3. *Encourage a healthy organization*, the features of which are discussed in detail later in this chapter (see pages 25–27). They certainly include voicing problems in the confidence that they will be tackled, and regular feedback between teachers, middle managers and top managers, both on a day-to-day basis and at summarizing occasions such as appraisal interviews.

4. *Acknowledge movement towards the values*, by giving encouragement, feedback and praise for actions which embody the new values. Encourage the values to be implicit in the targets set by every teacher and department. Conversely, firmly reject actions and targets which embody the old values. Be willing to sell or explain, but also try asking the teacher how the proposed target can be adapted to fit into the new values. The resulting discussion may result in other targets being set or may remove some false assumptions you were making about the original ones.

5. *Look for evidence* that the new values are being accepted. Try an attitude survey, interviewing, random group discussion, polling. Also, as

you move about the school or among those it serves, look for evidence of actions which embody the new ethos. Monitor its development and acceptance through affirmation and recognition.

A positive attitude to continuous improvement

Into the ethos of a school the head must build a positive attitude towards continuous improvement. Rates of improvement will not be evenly spread throughout the school and will vary over time, but the priority given to continuously seeking improvement is vital. Essentials in developing this positive attitude to continuous improvement are:

- Collection of real evidence on performance. As a consultant, I have helped schools to collect subjective and objective evidence to indicate progress in many aspects of school life, for example
  - numbers of parents opting into the school and their reasons for that choice. Where there were any opting out, their reasons for doing so were equally useful;
  - numbers of parents attending reporting evenings to discuss reports;
  - number and nature of complaints about the school from its customers – the parents – and equally the complimentary comments received;
  - attendance and lateness percentages for staff and pupils;
  - number and range of extracurricular activities and the percentage of pupils involved.

  These and other indicators should be made available to the staff. Without evidence the school cannot know how well it is doing and does not know where problems can be prevented and performance improved.
- Praise and credit for current achievements. Regular feedback and disclosure, as the appraising relationship demands, help to foster the necessary positive attitude towards improvement.
- Willingness to turn successful best practice into regular practice by recording it as the system of the organization. Ask those who handled a particular activity at the end of a session reviewing success, 'What do you feel could be improved in this activity and in the service it gave to its customers?' Record the system and the suggested improvements, to be used when the event is repeated. Not only will all the planning not need to be repeated, but the written record will already show how a repeat of the event can be improved.
- Expect staff to have the discipline to follow the recorded systems of the organization. There is little point in some teachers trying to develop 'best practice', if others slip back to previous habits. School systems are for all.

- Flexibility to enhance the system by adding improvements as they are recognized or engineered. Tradition has its positive aspects but be alert to the restriction and paralysis it can bring.
- Recognition for those who suggest changes which lead to an improved performance. Give public and private praise when anyone identifies an acceptable means of improving performance.
- Look for improving quality and raising customer satisfaction through improved systems and achieved targets.

Bringing about other changes in the school

A general strategy for managing change

Deciding on the change

If the decision on whether or how to change lies within the organization, use any appropriate decision-making technique such as algorithms, decision tree, means and ends analysis, etc. The same simple DO-IT approach runs through all such techniques:

- **D**efine the problem as precisely as possible.
- **O**pen your mind to as wide a range of possible solutions as you can.
- **I**dentify the best solution. Either, the option offering
  – the best outcome, or
  – the best of the worst scenarios, or
  – the lowest opportunity cost, or
  – the closest proximity to the most likely scenario
- **T**ake your decision.

Preparing for the change

Those managing the change must gain acceptance from those who are involved in implementing the change, in two ways. First, the managers of the change are sufficiently sound, professionally and technically, to carry out the change. Second, that the managers of the change have enough personal and interactive skills to listen to those implementing the change. The prospect of well-managed, confidently handled change in which the teacher's viewpoint will always be listened to and considered helps enormously in reducing the feeling of being a victim rather than a participating colleague. Other practical steps in preparation for the change are:

1. Interview all key personnel individually to explain the general principles of the change. Allow room in the plan for their contribution. Ask for their analysis of the change.

2. Design learning situations which will introduce staff to any new skills or techniques. A change of school ethos might require teachers to handle personal private interviews with parents or to standardize all marking or to handle record of achievement interviews with pupils. Any such situation might require new skills to be acquired or old ones to be refreshed. Covert fear of devaluing present skills or of facing new situations without the skills to handle them may make people appear to oppose the whole principle of a proposed change.

3. Make staff aware of any planned changes in management style. The changes may necessitate a change in management style within the organization. New values which stress quality performance may imply careful listening to, and discussion with, any teacher who has a point to make. A Japanese manufacturing firm which pioneered the practice of 'quality circles', has the maxim that 'everyone speaks' and expects full staff participation in the search for quality improvements. It is also possible that the style in which a change is introduced may not be the style in which it is proposed to run the resulting organization. Whatever the foreseeable style change, avoid misunderstanding and limit the culture shock by giving advance notice to staff.

4. Draw up a programme of the change which identifies key stages and activities. Publish the programme so that all concerned can see for themselves how well they and the organization are doing. Being up to date with schedule is a great motivator; those who fall behind can see this for themselves and make their own adjustments without the harassment of being chivvied along by senior management. Imagine playing in a bowling alley with a sheet hung between the bowler and the skittles and having to wait for the headteacher to appear to tell the teacher that the score is seven – or more likely that three have been missed! . How much more effective to be able to see one's own score and allow full play to professional self-improvement.

5. Review policies, procedures, organizational structures and job descriptions to check their compatibility with the change. New values may place greater emphasis on cross-curricular themes and create posts of cross-curricular responsibility. How will these relate in terms of task, authority, responsibility and procedure to existing posts of faculty responsibility and to senior management curricular responsibility? Preparatory review may save confusion and increase effectiveness.

Making the change more acceptable

1. Listen. Set aside time for personal private interviews for staff. Use your skills of open questioning, clarifying, summarizing, and of active

listening to understand how each person perceives the change. Encourage people to express the fears which underlie their reservations. Although teachers will be interested in the intellectual arguments which build to the academic case for the change as a whole, what concerns them more will be the change in their own role within the social system of the school. Encourage people to express these fears. These may come out as 'How will I be affected?', 'What's in it for me?' or 'How will I measure up to the change?' All these fears are better discussed than hidden.

2. Encourage identification with the change. Listen for the teacher's ideas on how the change could be improved. Stimulate the taking of some practical steps towards the change. Encourage people to stake out their own role in the change and in the resulting situation. Show those people who cannot yet see a function for their particular talents, how they can contribute and how their skills and experience will be used. Develop personal target-setting for high but achievable targets. But remember that this, in particular, is a time to be certain that the targets are realistic; failure can bring the change into disrepute while success will add momentum and increase identification with the change.

3. Show people how they gain. Listen particularly to those who feel they will lose by the change. Can this still be turned into a win–win situation by some concession which means much to them but may cost you little? If not, how can their sense of loss be minimized? Your aim is to avoid making anyone feel a victim of the change. When departmental or other team decisions are taken, aim to make it a decision of the whole group, a consensus rather than a majority decision. You need all staff working towards the change, not players and spectators.

Implementing the change

1. Begin the change as planned.
2. Monitor the actual change against the plan. Be alert to the danger of an informal system of values or practices developing, which is at odds with the formal; that is when the job actually being done in the school is far from what management believes is being done. Stay in touch with the change as it develops. Adjust the plan if this is appropriate. Review frequently to ensure that time, quality and activity forecasts are being met.

3. Celebrate achievement and publicize the progress. Encourage the feeling of a successful team moving towards planned targets.

Evaluating the change

1. Establish by comparison with the plan that the change was achieved.
2. Evaluate the change achieved against its fundamental aims. Did the change achieve its purpose? What was the cost in effort, time and good-will as well as in more objective measures? If it did not bring about the intended result, is a new plan for change needed?
3. Use the close monitoring which has been generated by this change, to build continuous review and appraisal as a permanent feature of the work of the school.

3
ORGANIZATIONAL CULTURE
MODELS

Some cultures are more likely than others to sustain the concept of the four essential elements of performance management: the creation of an appropriate culture , appropriate management, planned developmental experiences and continuous appraisal. Academic analyses of organizational cultures abound. Charles Handy (1976), while not referring particularly to school management, identifies four such cultures which, nevertheless, readily lend themselves as indicators of school culture. First, he has the power model with its spider's web organization where all structures and communication lines move radially from, or concentrically round, a powerful central leader. Handy's second model is one which relies heavily on excellent organization. It requires each member of staff to have a role, to be accountable by line management to a senior manager and thence to the head. A third culture is that called task, because the emphasis is placed not on a fixed line management but on teams created for specific purposes . The fourth is the person model in which the independent professional teacher is accountable only to his or her own conscience and treats the school as the kind of group practice in which doctors and solicitors frequently operate.

The power model

Teachers in schools which operate on this power model are quick to see that there will inevitably be a clash of cultures between that of their school and that required for flexible management, staff development and for the appraisal relationship. At their best the power model schools give staff accessibility to swift decision-making, clear, if imposed, targets and consistency of both vision and culture. At their worst, however, they are led by heads who reject or are out of touch with the needs of their pupils, their staff and their community. These heads do not have access to the open feedback of some other cultures. Establishing the culture for their school frequently took a tremendous amount of personal energy from them at a time when that culture, possibly, met the needs of the people for whom they were responsible. They do not want to consider changing that culture themselves, nor within their beliefs and values can they allow others on the staff to initiate or manage its change.

If the pace of externally imposed change becomes too fast, such a head may need to rely heavily on a trusted deputy to execute the changes while hanging on more determinedly than ever to those functions which there is no compulsion to alter. He or she cannot be wrong, will explain but does not expect to justify decisions and sees disagreement with a decision as disloyalty. Disloyalty means a rejection by the hierarchy as permanent as hell-fire. The problem with infallibility, however, is that you have to be right every time! Anne Jones (1987) aptly describes this culture as monarchic and points out how successful it was in some public schools and grammar schools. Though Jones describes this style as 'pre-comprehensive', she is as aware as any of us that it is still used in many smaller educational establishments, including comprehensive schools. In character such heads are usually clever, dominant and greatly respected by the local community.

The resulting organization may develop some of the following features:

- By controlling as many decisions as possible from the top, the head becomes a bottleneck delaying decisions for which the organization is waiting.
- Pleasing the head becomes a more important aim in the school than pleasing the clients.
- Problems and mistakes are regularly hidden from the hierarchy.
- Disagreement between staff results in bitter argument or takes the form of covert action and 'getting my own back' devices.
- The organization has a low capacity for change, and ends up as a stranded whale when the tide has ebbed.
- Staff tend not to seek or offer help. There is very little teamwork.
- Staff speak badly of one another and show little trust.
- The judgement of staff is generally not sought or respected outside their own immediate field of operation.

- Staff receive little feedback on their performance.
- Staff lack concern for one another; personal needs and feelings are not considered to be important.
- Staff feel undeveloped, stale and that their interest is not being sustained.
- The head tightly controls even small expenditures.
- Mistakes are never seen as an opportunity to learn.
- Poor performance is covered up.
- Tradition rules.

The bureaucratic model

The appraising school is likely to need very few features of Handy's (1976) second model, which Anne Jones (1987) calls the 'bureaucratic model'. Its positive features include job descriptions, determination of roles and an accountability structure. To comprehensive schools of the late '60s and early '70s such a management approach brought order out of chaos. Its weaknesses are that it was little more than a management technique for operating the power model. Based on 'management by objectives' with its downward cascading of tasks, it failed to tap into the experience, ingenuity and closeness to the action of the staff. The identification of problems and the details of their solution tended to arrive from above as part of the master plan. I can recall several schools of this culture where, for example, the timetable was produced like a rabbit from a hat each July, with little or no consultation during its construction.

The resulting organization may develop such features as:

- Heads make decisions with insufficient information and without advice. People complain about the irrationality of decisions.
- Staff see or can foresee things going wrong but do nothing about it. They walk past trouble and try to ignore it. 'It's not on my job description!'
- Staff guard their areas of job responsibility vigorously and aggressively.
- The head suffers from the 'lonely life' syndrome. His or her procedures are not carried out by staff as the head intended, even though there is great investment in administration.
- Staff receive little feedback on performance. If errors are discovered people blame each other or blame 'the system'.
- Staff feel bogged down in paperwork and procedures.
- Poor performance is tackled in a peremptory manner.
- Bureaucracy rules, even when structures, policies and procedures prevent the school from meeting the needs of its clients.

The task model

In many ways the task model is the bureaucratic model with in-built adaptability. When the bureaucratic model is set up in an organization its teams and structures are created to meet the needs of the time. But responsibilities and roles then become fossilized, and as the needs of society change, the school is less able to respond. It is the same weakness we saw in the power structure; a good school today will not be a good school tomorrow unless it builds in means of detecting the need for change and of delivering that change. This is why the appraising school of the 1990s admires some of the features of the task culture. The strengths of the task culture are its flexibility to deal with unforeseen change, the value it places on the abilities of all staff as team members and the acknowledgement that there are other, better solutions than the one the head might propose. Problems and solutions are expected to be dealt with close to the point of action.

One weakness in the task culture is the need for co-ordination and monitoring to ensure that parallel teams produce similarly fair solutions; for example, that there is even-handedness in the way pastoral teams treat children. Another is the traditional joke about working parties – that their dilatory pace kills many proposals. A third weakness is the tendency in such cultures for staff to come to believe that the working group is the only way of solving problems and making decisions.

The person model

The above three models each show a culture which recognizes the need for the existence of an organization. Staff in these schools expect to be managed towards the achievement of organizational goals, and 'the management' sees this as a definition of its task. The person model is different. It wants the individual's professional purposes to be paramount, and the management to provide the resources and support. Managers in such organizations are not higher in status than the professionals and have little control over them. When, some years ago, there was talk of appraisal in schools, one of the greatest obstacles seemed to be the aspect of school culture which said that one professional teacher could not observe, appraise or manage another. The head was seen as *primus inter pares* in professional matters, even if he or she did hold a figure-head responsibility. It was not only at the William Tyndale School that staff 'did their own thing'. Even in recent years, I have been a consultant to schools where giving feedback on performance to a fellow professional would be anathema to the staff.

The strengths of the person model are chiefly the importance which is restored to the role of the teacher, which can be lost in some of the earlier models, and the reminder to those who manage schools that one of their chief roles is to create the conditions in which good teachers can teach. Charles Handy (1984) reminds us that other professionals, when they form themselves into groups, do not 'talk of managers but of secretaries, bursars, chief clerk etc., indeed the managers of these organizations are always lower in status than the professionals'.

The weaknesses in the person culture, when a group of teachers wants to manage without systems and bosses, are recalled by Anne Jones (1987): 'Democracy took its toll; groups of staff fell out and broke off from the rest of the staff: getting so many individuals to agree what to do was time consuming, inefficient and often ineffectual.' In the end if it meant taking good teachers from the classroom and from the very work they were keen to do, the person culture in operation in schools is self–defeating.

Which of these models is most likely to be the culture for the appraising school? Let us remember that they are all caricatures of how schools are managed and their decisions are made. Few organizations carry out any of the models to perfection. Let us also remember that some features of all of these models appear in many schools with considerable success. The strong personal leadership of the power model, the essential organization and ac-countability of the bureaucratic model, the flexibility and respect for those lower down the hierarchy of the task model and the manner in which man-agement and administration serve the professional teacher in the person model. The appraising school must include all of these positive features.

The culture of the appraising school

Those who attempt the difficult task of analysing and describing the organ-izational culture of schools, have simplified the task for themselves by concentrating perhaps too heavily on management and decision-making. Some of the most powerful aspects of organizational culture are the effect of the culture on the staff and pupils of schools. Culture generates expecta-tions, attitudes and behaviour; it is the most powerful force developing that organization . In industry, positive culture is there in the company pride of IBM, of McDonald's and of Marks and Spencer. The powerful behavioural effect of culture is present in the appraising school when staff say such things as:

- 'I treated that parent with courtesy well below the standard expected here. I'll do better in future.'

- 'Thanks for working with me on the layout of the careers exhibition. By exploring all the possibilities together, I really believe we've come up with the best possible plan.'
- 'It seemed to me that the organization for the school musical was really good. Can you think of any possible way it could be improved?'
- 'I know it's not my responsibility, but it would reflect really badly on the school if I didn't stop now and resolve that incident.'

Such statements as these that show staff have understood the vision of the school and are consistently trying to maintain it. They show the vision to be widely shared and they show a strong flow of energy and action towards the achievement of that vision. Clearly, a healthy organization is one which has a strong sense of its own identity and mission, but has the capacity to adapt readily to change. What are the other features of the organizational culture of the appraising school in which all four key aspects of performance management will thrive? Its chief features are:

- People use a flexible leadership style, varying it according to the person and the situation.
- People generally know what is important to the school and what is not. They appreciate the vision and expect to interpret and work towards the strategic plan.
- There is a great sense of mutual responsibility. Individuals and teams contribute freely to policy and planning.
- People are not obsessed with status and role boundaries. Job descriptions are guides not strait jackets.
- Decisions are frequently made close to the action. People contribute to decision-making not merely on grounds of status, but more on the grounds of skill, knowledge and the need for personal and professional development. The judgement of junior staff is respected.
- People feel free to talk about their difficulties because they believe problems can be tackled and solved. Relationships and personal development are included in the discussion. People care about one another. When a crisis arises people work together to resolve it.
- People feel free to ask for help and free to give it. On-site personal and professional development is the norm and this, too, is freely given.
- People express pride in their own performance, the performance of their team and the performance of others in the organization. People expect to celebrate success and to confront poor performance.
- People are assertive but not aggressive in stating what they would like to happen. Conflicts are open, not hidden, and are considered to be a normal feature of development.

- Feedback on performance, progress reviews and appraisal are given and welcomed by all.
- There is a feeling that people really enjoy teaching and the related tasks. Top management do not leave their staff with impossible workloads but help to resolve priorities. The task of teachers seems manageable; people feel they are going for high but achievable targets.
- Policies, structures and practices are retained only so long as they help the school to achieve its vision. When they do not, they are replaced by others with greater relevance. All members of staff, not just those in senior posts, feel free to question and propose change and innovation.

These are some of the manifestations of the culture of the school in which performance management will most readily thrive. Such an organization is sensitive to culture creation and target-setting, sees staff development as an opportunity not a chore, uses flexible management styles to enhance teacher performance and believes that the appraising relationship is the appropriate day-to-day management contact between professionals.

4
TOTAL QUALITY

A new vision for schools

Many heads have said to me when I talk to them about the importance of a vision of the school, 'I accept what you say and I wish now that I had had this advice when I came first to this school. But it is too late now, I feel. What kind of vision could I now, suddenly, offer to the staff who have seen me accepting present performance for so long?' My reply is that there is no better climate to introduce a new vision than the present climate of change within the education system. Although the curriculum is more clearly and nationally identified today, schools and their staffs seem more than ever to be confused about target, direction and purpose in their working lives. Parents and administrators seem, too, to be urging schools to find a new motivation and to become somehow 'better', in a way they find hard to describe.

Yet the power for schools to manage their own resources and direct their use towards a vision they can call their own has never been greater. The vision which I can recommend is the vision of total quality. Total quality in education may be defined as the use of all activities, functions, features and characteristics of an organization to provide a service which satisfies the identified needs of customers. The two facets of quality performance are, therefore, the adaptation of the organization to provide an identified service and the extent to which that service appropriately meets the identified needs of customers. Quality management is management to ensure that the service a school offers is delivered as planned. This is achieved through managing the ethos of the school and through control of activities within it.

Characteristics of a quality system

Attitude

In a quality system an attitude runs throughout the school towards providing its clients with the best service the school can provide, both from its teachers individually and from its staff teams. Continuous improvement of the service is a maxim with everyone. Making the school the best by putting quality first is every teacher's aim. The attitude relates both to the provision of education for the students and to the satisfaction of the parents as customers.

Best practice

The system develops well-practised and documented routines which are continually being improved as the staff who operate them find new ways to upgrade the service or to cut time or other costs while maintaining the service. Quality is discussed regularly at quality circles, departmental target-setting meetings or at informal gatherings. The attitude which says 'We are an improving school', is obvious to all.

Remove the inhibitors

Management strives to limit the negative effects of the inhibitors of excellent teacher performance. These are such factors as unpleasant working conditions, ineffective school administration and poor school discipline. The culture of the school, as pioneered by top management, aims to leave the teacher to handle only the manageable minor pupil discipline issues, not to allow the maintenance of classroom order to dominate the teacher's task. Discipline is tackled by defence (removing graffiti and damage, responding to incidents) and by attack (planning to prevent misdemeanour, seeking out poor behaviour, publicizing detection). The appraising school aims to leave the teacher with an achievable task by creating 'the conditions in which teachers can teach' – first-class administration, positive working conditions and a level of pupil discipline which teachers can handle.

Power

Middle management has power and responsibility to change systems and reallocate resources to improve 'best practice'. Departments have freedom to find their own method of implementation of quality improvements, yet there is good co-ordination between the divisions within the school. Relating and co-operating in pursuit of excellence are basic skills of the middle manager.

Top management

Top management is committed to total quality and exhibits this. Top team members see themselves as serving the total quality movement and explicitly ask their staff how they can help to improve the quality of the service which teachers provide. Top management offers an example to staff in the quality of service which management provides for its teachers.

Training

Staff need to be developed in skills and ability and provided with the resources to produce a quality school. Begin with senior and middle management, who are instrumental in leading the change in practice and in attitude. Then, make teachers feel professional. Expect high standards. Train them in new skills which they can use in developing colleagues, meeting parents, solving problems and creating new structures. Make the conditions as professional as possible. Give people a professional responsibility. Teachers are professionals.

Praise and support

The atmosphere should be conducive to reporting mistakes, but the aim is to prevent recurrence rather than to blame. People who spot things going wrong are praised. Support is given to staff who are having difficulty achieving their target. Failures are seen as the seeds of improvement.

Feedback

Provide feedback on everything you see. Never leave people wondering what you thought about their performance, however small a part of their total programme. If you want people to move towards the vision, let them know for every step you see, whether it moves the school towards it or further away from it.

Search for improvement

People actively search for aspects of school life which could be improved. Easiest to find are areas where time and effort are being wasted; people closest to the action know this best. Suggestions for improvement are received positively. No improvement, however small, is derided. The attitude which will improve the school is one which seeks improvement after improvement. Train the senior management team into the habit of reviewing tasks. The weekly senior staff meeting is the place to do this. Have these two items on the fixed part of the agenda two items: 'What went well this week?' 'What went badly?' Maybe what went well was the examination entry procedure or parents' reporting evenings. Give praise there and then to the deputy responsible, but also ask senior staff if the event could have been improved. That way people learn the habit of 'improvement after improvement'.

Appraise and praise

Recognize not only the improvements which are being made but also those staff who suggested and implemented them. Publicize every improvement. Tell the staff concerned; tell the staff who were not involved. Tell pupils, parents and governors. Financial incentives are not necessary; it is sufficient for teachers to be working in an environment where they have some influence, can make improvements and have their contribution recognized. But be sure they are real improvements and never confuse this celebration, which is a form of praise for genuine progress, with the ballyhoo of image creation.

The effective school leader must create a befitting vision, present its key features as a mission statement and a strategic plan, and maintain the organizational culture in which the plan can develop. Appropriate management will help that vision to become a reality.

PART II
APPROPRIATE
MANAGEMENT

5
WHAT DO I HAVE TO DO?

The basic task in the appraising school

People in the appraising school know what their job is. They know what is the minimum performance level; it is written simply and clearly as the 'basic task' for all teachers. This basic task covers pastoral work, teaching, professional development, contributing to the organization as a whole and the administrative work of a teacher. Staff who have other specific responsibilities in excess of those of the basic task, such as managing others, administration of the school or managing resources, know what this additional work is and what is expected of them.

Confusion over the basic task

Though it is now usual in schools to describe in writing a teacher's additional responsibilities, many schools have still not clarified what is required as the basic task of a teacher. Frequently, in conducting a consultancy with teachers from a single school, I ask two groups of teachers to say what they believe their basic task to be. I ask them to identify the five chief areas which summarize the performance of a teacher in their school. The following are typical of the contrasting lists with which I am presented:

Group A	Group B
1. Preparing, teaching and assessing.	1. Examination results.
2. Understand the children in one's care.	2. Run a tutor group efficiently.

3. Extracurricular activities.   3. Administration.
4. Support and help in the   4. Professional development.
   department.
5. Liaison with parents.   5. Safety.

Teachers who believe that the school expects the group A definition as their basic task will operate differently and work to produce a different school from those in group B. Both groups could be working equally hard at what they believe to be their basic task but, for example, one group will see administration as part of the role of a teacher but will see extracurricular activities as an imposition. One group puts emphasis on the output of examination results while the other is more concerned with the quality of the input. In fact, teachers in one of the above groups had their description of the basic task very much in line with the implicit expectations of the management. Teachers in the other group were frequently receiving hints from the hierarchy about lack of diligence, not because they were lazy or incompetent, but because they had a developed a different concept of the basic task.

Basic task vs. job description

It is important that every teacher knows what the school requires of him or her. The usual method of conveying this information nowadays is by describing the job. A conventional layout for a job description is:

Title of the job:
  – position in the organization
Environment
  – location
  – facilities
Person the jobholder is accountable to:
People the jobholder is accountable for:
Overall purpose of the job:
  – objectives
  – manner of achievement
Duties and responsibilities:
Health and safety parameters
Remuneration
  – salary
  – allowances
  – likely changes
  – career structure

The job description should fall within the School Teachers' Pay and Conditions Document, issued under the Teachers, Pay and Conditions Act 1987.

Writing job descriptions has its dangers. Among all the detail required in a full job description there is every possibility that a succinct summary of the job and its purpose will be lost. Specifically, some dangers in the use of job descriptions are:

- Job descriptions tend to list all the tasks associated with a job without reference to their relative importance, time allocation or expected standard.
- Job descriptions frequently portray an idealistic description rather than a realistic one. They describe what would be done by an ideal teacher operating in an ideal school under ideal conditions.
- Job descriptions fail to keep pace with job changes. They tend to remain unaltered over long periods, perhaps because compiling them is so time consuming that regular reviewing seems a daunting task.
- Job descriptions tend to be regarded as maximum performance. They fossilize or become a strait-jacket. Robert Townsend (1970) calls job descriptions 'morale sappers', because they prevent people from keeping up with the changing nature of their job and from using their job to see how good they are.

How can these major disadvantages be avoided?

- By thinking about the purpose of a job when describing it and not being obsessed with its activities. This encourages people to ask 'Can we achieve this same purpose another way?' and 'How can we improve?' This thinking is essential to the development of a positive approach to total quality.
- By maintaining a constant dialogue between the teacher and the appraiser about the job. We are dealing with professionals, not robots.
- By including expected standards of performance and relative time allocations wherever possible. People need an answer to the question, 'How do I know when I've done it?'
- By deciding on an order in which to present the main tasks within any key result area, such as order of importance rather than frequency or chronology.
- By describing the minimum acceptable performance level and making it clear that this is so.
- By identifying the key areas of the job where results must be obtained if the organization is to be effective.

The resulting job description is concise and conveys the five or six key performance areas of the job. We have called this form of job description the basic task of a teacher, described in key result areas (KRAs).

Identifying the basic task

The basic task may be defined as 'that minimum level of individual performance which is required to allow the establishment to function satisfactorily' (see Figure 3). It is the responsibility of management to extrapolate from the mission statement of the school what is meant by 'satisfactory' and to produce the basic task. Its description should fall well within the duties and conditions of service set out for the first time ever in the School Teachers' Pay and Conditions Act 1987.

The basic task of a teacher should be so familiar that the teacher never has to wonder what it is. It should be so familiar that it provides the teacher with a short sharp answer to the question 'What am I here for?' It should be so familiar that the teacher can test any activity against the key result areas with the question 'Is what I am doing helping or hindering me in performing my basic task?' In fact, the opposite is often nearer the truth, and teachers are operating from a job description which gives no idea of which tasks are the 'Key' tasks that are vital to the running of a successful

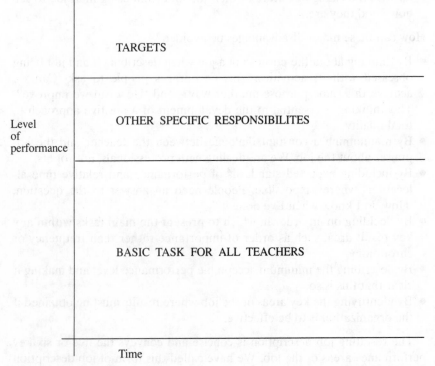

Figure 3   The basic task of the teacher.

school. In other schools there are not even job descriptions at all for teachers.

In both these cases – where there is no job description or where it gives no indication of key tasks – teachers inevitably make up their own mind about what is important and hope that what they are doing is what the school requires. Some guess wrongly and never discover why they are not considered to be good teachers. Some resent the reprimand they receive for failing to do properly a job which had not been made clear to them in the first place. Other teachers burn themselves out trying to be safe; they touch on as much as possible of an impossible job, regardless of its importance, because the school has not given them the opportunity to resolve priorities. We cannot even assume that because someone has been in post for a long time that he or she is clear about what is required. Even if they were clear five years ago, the priorities may have changed since then. Nor is it safe to assume that because you, as appraiser, know what your teachers should be doing that they will be able to read your mind. Only in a very few establishments do people have the opportunity to clarify what is expected of them or it is agreed what they have to do. Yet, it is an essential feature of the appraising relationship that teacher and appraiser can describe what the job is so that both know what is being appraised.

The need to define responsibilities before reviewing them became obvious to the six authorities on the School Teacher Appraisal Pilot Study in 1989, as it had to us at Warden Park School 15 years earlier. The Warden Park basic task is reproduced elsewhere (Trethowan, 1987), while the Steering Group of the Pilot Study selected the following aspects of performance for appraisal. In our terminology the following description represents the key result areas of the basic task of a teacher:

A.   THE TEACHER IN THE CLASSROOM
i.   Preparation
ii. Teaching skills
iii. Follow-up.

B.   THE TEACHER IN THE SCHOOL AND THE COMMUNITY
i.   Pastoral care
ii. Co-operation and teamwork
iii. Curriculum involvement.

C.   THE TEACHER AS MANAGER
i.   Management skills
ii. Leadership
iii. Self-determined professional development.

D.   THE TEACHER IN THE FUTURE
i.   Further training needed

   ii. Further experience needed
  iii. Potential for additional responsibility
  iv. Career aspirations.

The Pilot Report then lists certain 'trial' criteria which it felt may need modification in the light of experience gained during the pilot study. My advice as a consultant has been similar. Having helped schools to identify misunderstandings in what they believe to be the key result areas of the basic task, I stress the importance of negotiating and clarifying this perception. Make talking about the job a normal feature of the appraising relationship. Modification during the course of a year may be acceptable for a pilot project, but the school which is undertaking appraisal 'for real' needs to scotch the time-wasting and frustration which arise from a long-term misunderstanding of the basic task.

6
WHAT'S NEW ?

Target-setting in the appraising school

A target is a particular aspect of work agreed by appraiser and teacher to be raised to a high priority for achievement within a set period. A target may be:

- part of the basic task in which there is a shortfall in performance by the teacher (e.g. regular failure to meet record of achievement deadlines);
- a delegated part of the responsibility of the appraiser or of another teacher (e.g. to manage the finances of the department during the term of absence of the departmental head);
- a specifically nominated project (e.g. research the most suitable computer program on which to store departmental assessments);
- a personal one undertaken for the teacher's own professional development (e.g. chairing all departmental meetings for the year as an aspect of teacher development);
- a departmental or team one to be achieved by the group working co-operatively (e.g. to implement an effective equal opportunities policy in the department);
- a school one to be achieved by all staff operating together (e.g. to improve the quality of pupil discipline in the school).

In my experience over 90 per cent of targets are proposed by the teacher who will undertake the target. However, increasingly under LMS (local management of schools), a teacher is invited by the appraiser to take on a particular target for the sake of the organization. For example, a school may require a computerized adminiztration package to be tested and offers the project to the teacher as a target. Or the school may have lost its manager of the Duke of Edinburgh's Award scheme, cannot appoint a replacement and so asks a teacher to take it on as a target. The teacher is free to accept the challenge or to reject it. Usually, however, both before and after LMS, targets are proposed by the teachers undertaking them because they believe them to be useful in their own personal development or in the improvement of the quality of their own work, or because the teacher wishes to influence the development of the organization.

What is not acceptable in the appraising school is to criticize the teacher for not setting targets. We cannot define a minimum acceptable performance which we call the basic task and then discipline or disapprove of people for not agreeing to do more. The acceptable minimum cannot be unacceptable! Of course many teachers will do more. They will set targets and will expect confirmation that their targets have the support of the school. But those who only complete the basic task are doing the job they are hired to do and are entitled to respect for doing it.

How to form effective targets

1. Express them as end-results, not as processes or activities.
2. Express them as clearly as possible, avoiding ambiguity.
3. Agree them to be achievable within a stated time period.
4. Make them practical and feasible, not theoretical or idealistic.
5. Select only those which are important and of real consequence.
6. Make them precise, not too indefinite or too complex.
7. Express them singly; avoid combining targets.
8. Aim to stretch the target-holder personally or professionally.
9. Allow opportunity to redefine targets if circumstances alter.
10. Tailor the target to suit the person.
11. Relate the targets to the teacher's career plans where possible.
12. Aim to set four to six targets a year.
13. Agree their order of priority.
14. Agree the criteria for establishing success.
15. Agree targets to be realistic; do not aim too high or too low.
16. Encourage staff to develop through the challenge of high but achievable targets.

Examples of targets

When targets have been clearly described and agreed, when their priority, completion date and performance criteria have been established, staff can see for themselves when performance is falling below standard. Most teachers will then adjust their performance in order to reach the target. If they do not, then you, as appraiser, will tell them that you too have noticed, and this leads naturally to a discussion to resolve the shortfall.

In practice, actual targets which teachers set focus mainly on three areas:

1. Improvement of performance in the present post, e.g.
   - create suitable additional material from the English course, for use with lower sets;
   - create more situations for group activity and discussion in the tutor group;
   - change the organization of last year's City and Guilds course in order to keep a better record of completed work.
   - be better organized by attempting to complete reports and marking well in advance of the due date.
2. Personal and professional development, e.g.
   - become proficient at using the word processor;
   - gain experience of teaching geography;
   - continue working on the school timetable with the deputy head;
   - accept some delegated tasks from the faculty head as preparation for a similar post elsewhere;
   - continue as an efficient deputy head of Moorland House and maintain my candidacy for any future head of house vacancy.
3. Development of the department or school in the future, e.g.
   - introduce economics as a GCSE option subject;
   - launch a successful BIS (Business and Information Studies) course;
   - develop material for a skills-based module in history for year 8;
   - discuss and agree a strategic plan for the introduction of core skills into 16–18 A and AS level work in the humanities faculty.

The cycle of target-setting and review is most frequently the same as an academic year, running from one June to the next; this allows the period from June to September for preparation of and adjustment to the new targets. This cycle also necessitates the review of external examination statistics at a time other than at the performance review; this is an excellent feature, since such results tend to swamp other important aspects of performance if they are not discussed separately. The external examination review of results can then take place in September.

Why use target-setting?

Target-setting is a practice which the appraising school must develop. It encourages the habit of undertaking clearly defined tasks with equally clear performance criteria. Asking 'How will I know when I've done it?', becomes normal practice. It has benefits for the teacher and the school.

Target benefits for teachers include:

- the opportunity to influence the development of the organization by playing a part in that development;
- the opportunity to feel that their performance matters in the school;
- the assurance that work being tackled is the work the organization requires;
- the confirmation that their work is being recognized;
- the assurance that a record of high performance is being kept which can be used in reference writing and in promotion reviews or in career development discussions.

Target benefits for the organization include:

- the opportunity to obtain from teachers close to the points of implementation their identification of school and staff development needs;
- the opportunity to be sure that the teacher is aware of those targets which the school expects him or her to achieve;
- the opportunity to show the teacher that his or her performance genuinely matters to the school;
- the opportunity to motivate the teacher when informed praise is given for good performance;
- the opportunity to motivate teachers to improve when informed criticism of performance can be given;
- the opportunity to identify and and tackle problem areas and poor performance;
- the opportunity to know accurately which teachers have which weaknesses. Ill-formed personal judgements are replaced by open appraisals;
- the opportunity for teachers to provide feedback on the strengths and weaknesses of the appraiser's performance, either to the appraiser or to the appraiser's manager at a 'leapfrog' interview;
- the opportunity to take from the teacher the pressure of not knowing which of the interest groups surrounding the school to aim to please. The basic task and targets as agreed with the appraiser are the clear objective;
- the opportunity to manage change through targets agreed with departments and individuals and to monitor that change.

7
TO WHOM AM I ACCOUNTABLE?

My manager is my appraiser

In the appraising school people know who their appraiser is: their appraiser is the person who is responsible for their performance – their manager. It is with this person that they agree what they have to do – the person with whom they negotiate their targets. It is this person to whom they turn to discuss priorities when they are being asked to do several things at the same time. It is from this person that they can expect a word of praise when things go well. For most secondary school teachers this person is their Head of Department. For most heads of department it is one of the deputy headteachers. For secondary school deputy headteachers and often for the whole staff team in a primary school it is the headteacher. That person is responsible for the performance of the people he or she manages, agrees with them what is important, encourages them, supports them, agrees to the provision of resources, facilitates their working, develops them and appraises them. Hundreds of primary schools already operate in this way, as do many departmental heads in secondary schools.

Questions and answers on the appraiser

People who do not understand the essential relationship between appraiser and teacher in the appraising school ask such questions as:

- 'Can I choose my own appraiser?'
  'No', says the appraising school; it has to be the person who is responsible for your performance. The opinion of a valued colleague, a

respected friend or a sensitive sage might give useful perspectives on your performance or your potential. But those people are not able to agree tasks, standards and targets. Their comments can be an important preparation for the appraisal. But what they offer can never be 'feedback with responsibility', which is another definition of active appraisal.

- 'Can the appraiser be an impartial outsider – someone from another school, a local adviser, a national inspector?

  'No', says the appraising school; it has to be someone who manages your performance from day-to-day. The appraising manager works close to his or her people, helps to prioritize their workload, gives day-to-day feedback and does the explaining and coaching which are part of good staff development. Popping in occasionally to see a lesson or discuss a project does not give a broad enough view of a teacher's total performance even in the basic task, let alone in agreed, relevant and developmental target areas. Appraisal is only meaningful if it takes place within a continuous appraising relationship.

- 'Can my headteacher be my appraiser?'.

  'Yes', says the appraising school, if the head has a team of fewer than about eight people to appraise. Many primary schools fit this pattern. A secondary school head could have ten times as many teachers on the staff, many of them teaching subjects in which the head could offer little personal advice or support. The appraiser needs to be someone close to the action, who appreciates the particular difficulty of teaching this subject to this class at this time. The best appraisal roles for the head of a large school are, first, as appraiser of the performance of members of the senior management team, and second, as leapfrog appraiser for staff who want to review an appraisal they have already experienced.

How the appraiser helps to relieve stress

Far from causing or maintaining stress in teachers, an appraising relationship is an established means of containing and relieving stress levels. Appraisal gives the teacher:

- a person with whom to discuss personal or professional problems;
- a person close to the teacher's work situation who is aware of the conditions under which the teacher operates;
- an experienced professional who shares the responsibility for the teacher's performance;
- a source of information which is related specifically to the work of the teacher;

- a source of feedback who can recognize and praise achievement;
- a manager with whom to adjust work expectations and targets to an achievable level;
- someone with whom to communicate and who has authority to make changes in departmental conditions and to represent the teacher's case with top management, if necessary;
- a source of support and advice;
- an experienced colleague who is responsible for the development and training of the teacher for present and future posts;
- someone with whom to share worries and concerns.

An appraising relationship can mean someone to whom the teacher can talk, who listens, who understands the teacher and his or her situation, who is responsible for the teacher's performance and has authority to adjust some of the pressures being experienced. All of these features of the appraising relationship help to relieve stress.

We now have the basics to begin an appraising relationship. Teachers know what they have to do, they know why they are doing it, they know how to prioritize by using the key result areas, they know how to use the target-setting process as an opportunity to show how good they are. They know with whom to relate on a day-to-day basis and for a periodic review of performance. They know where to turn for clarification, explanation and discussion of general work problems as well as for advice, coaching and development.

8

MAKING SUCCESSFUL APPOINTMENTS

Job analysis

The beginning of successful staff development is wise appointing. The whole process of staff management starts with this step, which is vital to the success of the appraising school. Who has not heard a similar remark to that of the head who said to me, 'I made a serious mistake when I picked that teacher. I've regretted it for years.' Yet the appointment was made with little analysis or preparation and nothing was learned from the error.

When a vacancy occurs the appraising school, in the light of its strategic plan, considers the purpose of the job. It asks:

- What is the purpose of this job?
- Do we need this job at all? Is this a purpose we are still aiming to achieve?
- Are there other ways of achieving it than by a replacement to this post?
- Can the responsibilities of this post be subsumed into any other post or can this post absorb other responsibilities?
- Are there other ways in which costs can be reduced on this post; for example, should grade of post be revised?

The appraising school will not lose any opportunity to ensure that practices keep pace with purposes. It will ask the departing teacher, the appraiser and those who interact with them to consider, in relation to the vacant post, its purposes, responsibilities, activities and the factors which affect performance in the job. A consultant or an appropriate LEA adviser might be called in to help with, or to focus objectively on, these deliberations.

The person specification

Once agreement is reached on the analysis and grade of the post the appraiser, as manager of the post, should produce the job description, based on the work of an academic year or the usual cycle of the job. It may be that the existing job description has been kept up to date through continuing discussions of the basic task and its key result areas. But it may equally well be the case that the job analysis and ensuing discussion have necessitated a new job description.

Table 1   Person specification.

Job title: Teacher of science
Job pay grade: MPG

Attributes	Essential	Desirable	Undesirable
Physical make-up	Good general health Clear speech	Non-smoker	
Attainments	Degree in a science subject Able to teach balanced science	PGCE in science subjects GCE A level in maths	Chemistry qualification (two already in dept)
General intelligence	Able to take initiative Sound common sense	Able to develop new schemes	
Special aptitudes	Good organization and class control Able to lead on biology topics	Botany and biology	Desire to teach chemistry at A level
Interests		Conservation Field work	
Disposition	Good team-worker Relates well	Keen to plan new courses and assessments	
Circumstances	Stable Living in the area or willing to set up in the locality		

The next step is to write a person specification. Experience shows this to be the most likely stage to be omitted. Its main purpose is to open up the thinking on the kind of candidate who could fill this post. It brings pre-judice out into the open, clears the mind of preconceptions and discourages stereotyping. An example of a person specification for a specific teaching post is given in Table 1, but essentially a person specification reminds the school of all the significant characteristics required for the performance of this job. It requires the school to consider whether those characteristics are essential minimum criteria or are desirable optional extras for the post. It also requires the school to decide if there are any characteristics which are unacceptable and are therefore disqualifications for the post. Such agree-ment will prevent the appointment of a teacher on pure chance factors – the one who 'Looks a lot like Jack, and you know how good Jack was!' Be sure, though, that the criteria which feature as essential really are essential to that post. The criterion 'Must be a biology graduate' may be pure tradition when a wider appreciation of science may be not only sufficient but also more appropriate.

If you are now freed from using the LEA application form, look at the possibility of designing your own. Given a generic one for the school it is not too difficult to adapt it for a particular post, especially in view of modern desk-top publishing facilities. The more relevant the information you can collate on the applicants, the better will be your selection.

Selection

After appropriate advertising, distribution of application forms and the 'further details' information, taking up references, shortlisting (following longlisting if there are enough candidates) and inviting the candidates to interview, there are still some key steps to remember:

1. Give the selectors something other than an interview to inform their judgement. Interviews favour the talker at the expense of the doer. Restore the balance for the practical candidate by including an aptitude test, a simulation or a live exercise. Score the results and use the infor-mation alongside that gleaned in interview. Read Hall Mackay and Morgan (1986) on this in relation to headship interviews and adapt for other school posts.

2. An interview is a vehicle for two-way communication to allow the inter-change of information so that appropriate future courses of action can be decided on. That definition applies to all interviewing – performance ap-praisal, grievance resolution, discipline, exit interviews and selection inter-

views. Guidance in performance appraisal interviewing appears later in this book (see Part IV), and the basic skills of questioning and listening which are discussed there are also the prerequisites for successful selection interviewing. Use the 70:30 rule to remind yourself that the interviewer should talk for 30 per cent or less of the interview time. We know these rules, we have these skills but we forget them as soon as an interview begins.

3. Ideally governors would leave the job of staff selection entirely to those people who are going to set targets, and develop, manage and appraise the staff they select. If, as a head of department, my performance is to be judged on the results of the people I manage, then I want the best I can get. If governors want to be involved, get the headteacher to agree with the governing body that only those governors who are trained in interview skills and willing to give the time to the whole selection exercise can be considered for an interviewing role. Before LMS, thousands of school interviews were rushed trying to balance the diaries of governors, LEA officials and the headteacher.

4. Never allow into the role of interviewer a person who has not prepared for it. A pre-interview session at which the job analysis, job description and the person specification are explained and discussed is essential. These two rules, about training and pre-interview planning, should be agreed with the governors as fundamental.

5. Panel interviews are for window dressing and rubber stamping. If you have to use them, make sure that each panel member has assigned responsibilities to research and question and that each records his or her preferences at the end of the interviews before pooling their opinions. Whether or not your school needs its showpieces, make sure that the real interviewing is undertaken one to one. The cornerstone interview which carries most weight has to be the one between the candidate and his or her future appraiser. This one-to-one appraising relationship is at the heart of the target-setting, development, management and appraisal of the appraising school. Let it start working at the interview, even before the appointment is made. Other people of valued judgement will also interview the shortlisted candidates and their doubts, if they have any, about the appraiser's choice will make the appraiser think hard. But the appraising school backs the appraiser's judgement. If you have serious doubts about the judgement of the person to whom the appointed teacher will be accountable, that person should not be in the post, let alone taking a leading part in staff appointments.

6. Play the percentage game. You are more likely to select the best candidate when being guided by your agreed person specification than by using that innate talent you believe you have for picking winners. That

same document will help you avoid prejudice, discrimination and subjective considerations which may otherwise creep into selection decisions.

7. Be prepared to appoint a candidate with the potential to be trained and developed on the job. Willingness and ability are the key factors, not experience and qualification. Accepting the under-experienced or underqualified often enables the selection of more able candidates, happy to stay longer and possibly on a lower salary than an experienced, off-the-peg candidate who has trained for your post in the practices and ethos of another organization.

8. Limit the danger of selection decisions taken under pressure of an interview by not cramming one 20-minute interview between two other 20-minute interviews. Show respect for the candidates by inviting them at different times and days and by not asking them to wait while you reach an unnecessarily pressurized decision. The appraising school respects its guests and values the impression it makes on them.

9. Be willing to invest time in this vital process. Review how much time is spent on staff selection. Fifteen hours' work, from advertisement to interview, does not seem an unreasonable amount of time to devote to selecting a teacher, but few schools spend half that much on the exercise. We all know that staff selection is a vital activity but he devote less time to it than we profess.

Induction of new staff

Following the appointment of a new teacher, the appraiser should implement an induction process to draw the teacher into the organizational culture of the school. A planned induction into becoming effective within the culture of the organization is necessary, regardless of the seniority of the teacher. The induction must cover more than a description of the basic task, of the people and procedures which facilitate the smooth running of the school. It must help the teacher to develop or recall the skills for the post – from appropriate disciplining of children to conducting a record of achievement interview or meeting an angry parent. Relationships and attitudes are also part of an induction programme – the accepted relationship between children, between staff and between departments, those attitudes which consciously contribute to developing the culture of the organization. The appraising school will have identified the ethos it wants to develop and the attitudes most likely to help that development. By providing a planned induction the school will not miss the best opportunity of all of familiarizing newly arrived teachers with the knowledge, skills and attitudes which will make them more quickly effective.

It is important that the responsibility for delivering this programme lies with someone to whom its success matters. There are few people in the school to whom it matters more than to the teacher's appraiser – the person who manages, works with the teacher and is accountable for the teacher's performance. In most cases this appraiser will be a middle manager, probably a head of department. However, the responsibility for managing and co-ordinating the total induction programme should be with an induction co-ordinator, probably a senior member of staff. This co-ordinator will also arrange the delivery of those parts of the programme which can be centralized. That centralized programme will present items common to all new staff, such as

- school systems;
- school philosophy;
- collecting feedback on the induction programme;
- meeting senior staff.

The appraiser, meanwhile, delivers the more personal, local part of the programme, such as:

- meeting departmental and pastoral colleagues;
- personal timetable details;
- department routines and practices, including appraisal;
- departmental administration, assessing and reporting;
- building the appraising relationship;

One of the key features of a successful induction programme is its pacing. Inevitably, induction begins with the selection interview – its documentation, planning and the interview itself. The appraising school is already showing candidates how it values people by the way it invites them for interview and treats them when they accept. Another important stage is the period between appointment at the selection interview and taking up the post. An early mistake we made in the school I led was to use this stage to collect together all the printed information about the school – timetable, staff handbook, parents' brochure, class lists, etc. – and sent it to our newly appointed staff. We gave no guidance on its relative importance or priority and consequently it was not a successful practice. It gave 'information indigestion' to those who tried to read it all. It told them something about the school, too. 'Here is a well organized school,' it implied, 'which does not spend time seeing things from the viewpoint of the teacher.'

A team of experienced managers from Shell Oil encouraged us to look at things differently. On their advice we listened to those who experienced the programme and to those who knew which information was important to have at different times during the induction period We paced the programme of knowledge and skills throughout the year. Immediately the programme became more successful. But it did something equally important: it showed attitude and values in a way that a memo on the subject could never have done.

One final feature of a good induction programme is the opportunity it builds into itself for feedback and assessment. Those who experienced the programme and those who manage it need to assess not only whether it conveys information skills and attitudes in a timely and thorough manner, but also whether it exhibits a caring concern for the teacher. Does the programme ease the teacher into an appraising relationship in an appraising school?

9
MANAGEMENT STYLE AND THE APPRAISING RELATIONSHIP

Management style descriptors

How do staff manage each other in the appraising school? An appraiser's natural style comes from his or her background, personality, the example of earlier leaders and a range of random factors. But this 'way of relating to people' which we call 'style' has such an impact on teacher performance that it is far too important to leave to chance historical factors.

The day-to-day style which the appraiser aims to develop depends on three groups of factors, which are here called 'forces'. These are:

1. Forces in the situation, such as the amount of time pressure or whether the problem to be solved is open ended or a straight choice between alternatives.
2. Forces in the leader, such as natural style, value system, confidence, security and the basis of his or her power.
3. Forces in the follower, such as the ability and willingness of the follower and the shared expectation which exists for development and training.

As a headmaster I searched for years for a model of management which was sufficiently realistic for me to use as an analysis of the everyday leadership actions of those teachers who managed others in the school. Most models had the weakness that they seemed to be suggesting that there was an ideal style towards which all managers should strive, when it was patently obvious from managing in real life that the style used by good managers varied with the situation – even sometimes when dealing with the same person. The Paul Hersey and Ken Blanchard (1982) Situational Leadership model, however, answered all my reservations. I was introduced to this management model as a member of a 'Style and Performance' course for IBM managers – the first headteacher to have such an experience. As quickly as possible afterwards, all middle and senior managers on the school staff were introduced to it and thereby given not only an incomparable appreciation and understanding of management, but a shared management language in which to communicate. I offered it on courses for other headteachers and found the same ready acceptance of its close relationship with good practice and with common sense.

The simplification of the Hersey and Blanchard model offered here has come about through years of its use. Their original work, *Management of Organizational Behaviour: Utilizing Human Resources* (Hersey and Blanchard, 1982), should be required reading on all school management courses. From experience and from the Hersey and Blanchard model, the simplest effective analysis of styles is:

Tell – Telling includes explaining, informing, instructing, describing, detailing, delineating, deadlining, demanding, announcing, directing, guiding, correcting, clarifying and indicating priorities in a job.

Sell – Selling includes persuading, coaxing, coaching, encouraging, convincing, getting something accepted and winning someone over.

Participate – Participating includes discussing, sharing ideas, negotiating, bargaining, seeking the other person's viewpoint, pooling ideas and all forms of co-operative planning.

Delegate – Delegating includes authorizing, trusting, devolving, assigning and empowering others to act on their own initiative.

Teachers can readily identify these styles being used daily in their schools, either by them or on them. For example, one head of house says: 'I use the tell style with a certain form tutor who is unwilling to meet deadlines. I use the selling style when encouraging form tutors to review pupils regularly. I use a participating style when helping subject teachers devise strategies for dealing with difficult pupils. I use delegation when I allow form tutors who have good relationships with their pupils to deal with pupil problems.'

A head of faculty says: 'In the tell style I define the deadlines that have to be met and I state when we will have meetings. I feel I am using the sell style when I present to staff the need to keep accurate records and in convincing them of how I would like the faculty to develop in the future. I negotiate and get active participation from all the faculty in developing the new schemes of work that we are developing for Key Stage 3 and the new syllabus. After that stage, many staff have volunteered to develop worksheets, diaries, etc. and they then continue on their own, in delegation.'

Another teacher, a head of faculty, can see the same pattern in the styles in which she is managed. 'I am managed in the tell style in the definite instructions which come from the head, deputy head or head of year, as I am a year tutor, for example regarding attendance at assembly, register deadlines, etc. I am encouraged in the sell style by the deputy head to keep an accurate record of expenditure from the department budget in the way that he prefers. I am invited to negotiate and participate in negotiating timetable requirements for the coming year. The future plans for the faculty are delegated to me and I am asked by the head to formulate the way that our faculty will be going in the near future.'

Using styles appropriately

Seeing these styles described, most appraisers will recognize that their order is significant, since that sequence indicates a decrease in the control exercised by the appraiser and an increase in the teacher's freedom and authority to act (see Figure 4). Most appraisers also recognize that they probably use the full range of all four styles in the course of a work cycle in

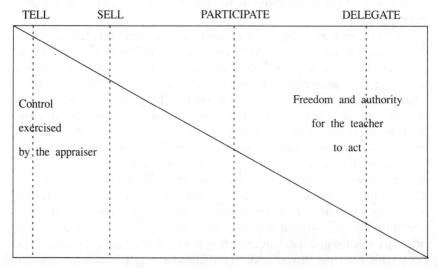

Figure 4 Styles and freedom for the teacher to act.

school. The skill in using these styles is to use them in the appropriate situation to maximize the effectiveness of the appraiser's management relationship. In other words, you should not be 'telling' when 'participation' is needed nor trying to delegate to a teacher who is confused and needs the support and encouragement of the 'selling' style.

Decide which style to use according to the effectiveness of the teacher in performing the specific task under consideration. Consider effectiveness to be comprised of two key factors.

- Expertise: professional knowledge and skills (what Hersey and Blanchard (1982) call 'ability').
- Orientation: attitude, confidence and commitment (what Hersey and Blanchard (1982) call 'willingness').

If, as appraiser, you believe the teacher to be low in either of these respects in relation to a particular task, then use either the tell or the sell style. But if you would rate the teacher highly in both, then use participation or delegation. If in doubt, err on the side of an over-estimate of effectiveness. With an over-estimation which to be wrong the teacher will fail to respond and the appraiser drops back one style from, for example, participating and sharing in making a departmental decision to selling the appraiser's own decision when the teacher lacks the expertise or the attitude to participate. If the original estimate was well wide of the mark and the sell style also fails to draw the appropriate action from the teacher, then moving farther back along the continuum, the tell style becomes the only possible course of action.

Under-estimation of expertise or orientation in managing the teacher is dangerous. Try managing in the tell style a deputy head who is confident, experienced and skilled in school timetable construction and who is willing to accept that delegated task. Imagine the reaction of the deputy head when you announce that in future you will be telling him or her what to do, step by step; no action is to taken without you having initiated it. Imagine the frustration for the deputy head as he or she waits to be told what to do next while knowing exactly what has to be done. Frustration will lead either to conflict or, what is worse, to the deputy dropping back in attitude and commitment to match the style in which he or she is being managed. The willingness which had previously made the deputy head so effective will disappear. The deputy will appear angry, antagonistic, sulky, critical, unwilling or lazy. Almost unbelievably, along with the deterioration in orientation will come the deliberate loss of expertise. 'Right,' I can hear the deputy head saying. 'If you want to tell me what has to be done every step of the way, don't expect any initiative from me. I'm going to sit here and wait to be told what to do next. Treat me as if I know nothing about timetables and I'll behave as if I know nothing about timetables!' This is staff development in reverse – the active de-skilling of teachers.

This example illustrates the powerful effect of style on performance. How many of the unco-operative, obstructive, unskilled and uninterested teachers who exist on any school staff have become that way in reaction to the style in which they have been managed? Could the school have handled and developed them differently? Would their effectiveness now be greater if a more suitable style had been used? Performance management in the appraising school implies a constant search for the appropriate style – the style which maximizes not only teacher performance but teacher development as well.

The tell style

The tell style is most appropriate when either expertise or orientation is low. Expertise is low when the teacher lacks the knowledge, information or general know-how to carry out a specific job, for example when a teacher is new to the profession, to a school, to a post or to a task. Telling in these cases is providing information, giving direction and explaining requirements. As a consultant, I frequently see examples of situations calling for the the appropriate use of the tell style. I continue to meet teachers who are frustrated in their attempt to be effective because they do not know the answers to simple operational questions and seek to be told. For example,

- What is the deadline for this report?
- Am I expected to make direct contact with outside agencies?
- What information is required from my visits to primary schools?
- Who is responsible for producing the option handbook?
- What are the planned meetings for the school year?

If I know that when I lack information or knowledge to perform my job well, I will be given those data or will be shown the standard required, I am reassured. If I know that as I perform a task, if it becomes apparent that I lack some skill or ability my appraiser will make me aware, will give me the know-how and will see it as part of my development, then that too is reassuring. This is the tell style in relation to low expertise.

Orientation is low when the teacher is so lacking in commitment that his or her performance is falling below a previously agreed standard for the job. Though instances are less common, equally in need of a tell style are teachers who decide not to achieve the basic task – the form tutor who refuses to meet deadlines, the teacher who will not allow a colleague to observe lessons, the head of department who will not review the staff teaching record books of the department, the head of year who will not hold regular tutor meetings. As the ineffectiveness of the other styles of management becomes apparent, all the above examples require the use of the tell style. Tell the teacher what is required and what are the consequences of continued failure to meet that requirement. If, because a teacher lacks commitment, he or she fail to treat pupils with respect by ignoring their homework assignments, then it may be reassuring to know that someone cares enough to tell the teacher. But even if it is not reassuring, he or she will find it difficult to argue that it is not appropriate. In the appraising relationship, there is a clear role for the tell style.

The dangers with the continual use of the tell style are:

● Because of its apparent speed of delivery it can become a habit. As a habit, it may lead to the inappropriate use of the style in situations where the teacher is knowledgeable, willing and skilled and has an equally valid viewpoint to offer.
● It applies a brake to the development of the teacher who becomes passive under this style, accepting the appraiser's judgement in every situation.
● Because it frequently begins with the direct presentation of a viewpoint or evaluation rather than a shared analysis of a problem, there is a risk of polarized views leading to conflict and deteriorating relationships.
● It serves as a poor model for organizational development since it takes downward communication into account, but gives little weight to communication in any other direction.

Bear in mind that the tell style relates to a specific task. An otherwise competent and experienced head of mathematics who takes on the task of timetable writing will need to be told about priorities, procedures, practices, etc. Beware of believing that because someone is experienced enough to handle delegation in one field that there is never a case for telling, instructing or directing in another.

One final feature of this telling style as used in the appraising school is important. Telling is not yelling. Yelling is turning a shortfall in performance into a major incident; it is aggressive. Telling means making the teacher aware of the appraiser's perception of the performance; it leads to staff development.

The sell style

The sell style is used to provide the teacher with the appraiser's specific perception of performance, to provide an opportunity for clarification, in order to gain the teacher's acceptance of the perception and have the teacher agree to develop on the proposed lines. It says: 'I know what I want you to do, but I want to coach you if you lack the expertise and to coax you if you lack the orientation to do it.' It is appropriately used at relatively low levels of expertise and orientation, but not at levels which are so low as to make telling appropriate. In England and Wales recently, teacher expertise levels have fallen because new National Curriculum syllabus requirements, assessment procedures and record of achievement interviewing techniques have left teachers requiring new skills and unsure of the usefulness of their existing ones. The selling style with its coaching, supporting and encouraging of staff to develop new skills and to re-align their existing ones has been appropriately evident.

But educational changes have arrived in such an order and at such a speed that the willingness and confidence of staff have also fallen. Where delegation and participation had been appropriate styles a year or two ago, now, with the general change in orientation, the coaxing, persuading and winning over of colleagues, which are other facets of the selling style, have been in frequent use. As a consultant I see the burden of this relationship-intense style being borne by middle managers, particularly as they try to convince their teams to give more than the basic task requirement, to make the changes effective.

The dangers with the selling style are similar to those of the tell style in that it does not encourage staff maturity and growth. It implies that the seller uses effective persuasion techniques and so wants to know the teacher's views, but only to help the seller to present his or her views more convincingly to the teacher. In reality it pays scant attention to the teacher's views. It can also rely particularly heavily on appraisers having something to offer in exchange for compliance – from safe-guarded 'free' periods to the possibility of promoted posts. When selling has had no reward to offer and has had to rely on charisma, this quality has frequently worn thin. In the appraising school people respect the listener and believe that the most persuasive argument to use with the selling style is a good and well-presented case.

There is one other important use for the selling style in the appraising school. This style is used to deliver staff coaching within the staff development role of total performance management. Since coaching is a form of tutoring which relies heavily on training a teacher in a particular mode of operating, it is closely akin to the selling style. In the same way that a tennis coach sells the skills of returning a serve, so there are skills in which the teacher can be coached. It is of little use merely telling a teacher to improve interpersonal skills; such skills are developed by demonstration and intensive encouragement. 'Don't just tell me,' the teacher says to the appraiser, 'Stay with me, show me, work with me until I have taken on board the skill that you have and I at present patently do not have.' Time intensive as it is, it is another form of the essential flexible management style used in the appraising school.

The participative style

The participative style lays emphasis on exchanging perceptions and on shared decision-making between appraiser and teacher. The appraiser aims to be seen as a support, so encouraging the teacher to identify his or her own difficulties or those of the situation and to propose solutions. The participative style is most appropriate with teachers who are fairly high in the appropriate aspects of expertise – probably experienced, knowledgeable and skilled and aware of their objectives and how to achieve them. Teachers who are effectively managed in this style also need to be fairly positively orientated – confident, committed and willing to work on their clarified tasks. If they are not, the appraiser will find it necessary to drop back into the tell or sell styles. Examples of situations for which participation is suitable are:

- Most appraisal interviews, since the teacher has the experience of having worked through the year which is being appraised.
- A teacher who has just completed an induction year being asked to help with the planning of next year's induction programme.
- A teacher who finds he or she is overloaded with simultaneous tasks because their timing has been badly planned expects to talk through the problem and solution with the appraiser.
- Normally when working with any teacher on a task in which that teacher will be involved in the future. If the teacher would prefer to be told what to do then do just that; the teacher is indicating the level of expertise or of willingness and is asking to be managed appropriately.

The participative style focuses attention not on perpetuating hierarchical judgement, but on issues and interests to be discussed as between equals. The head who says to his senior management team 'I've made a decision. I'd like to have your reaction to it.' is not using participation, but is selling. The participative style requires an open mind to receive every idea it can about how to improve the school and its performance. It is a style which seeks to involve people as much as possible in decision-making. The participative style stimulates the teacher's initiative, but allows both appraiser and teacher to learn each time it is exercised. It is another excellent form of on-the-job training. Though expensive in time when compared with the tell style, it allows teachers to talk through many proposals and then put one of them into practice, having agreed an appropriate level of support. No off-site course, however good its simulation techniques, can quite match this as a developmental experience.

There are very few dangers with using this style as long as the appraiser is an observant listener with sufficient skill to change to a more directive style if that becomes necessary. It is much better to pay the teacher the compliment of beginning in this participative manner and moving to a tell style when that seems more appropriate, than to use the tell style on a teacher who is able and willing to participate with the appraiser in the search for the best solution to a problem. The appraising school aims to develop the ability and willingness of its teachers at least to the stage where participation is the appropriate style in which to manage them.

The delegating style

This style gives the teacher responsibility for his or her own work, for analysing problems, deciding what to do about them and for implementing those decisions. The appraising school uses this style with teachers who have agreed with the appraiser what their job is, have the knowledge and skill to tackle it and have the confidence and enthusiasm to complete it. Such teachers rarely need to talk through problems, and while they welcome the interest of the appraiser they do not need to think of him or her as a form of regular, active support.

There are risks in an appraiser adopting this style. Since difficulties are only rarely jointly identified and resolved, the teacher frequently finds his or her own solution to problems. John, an able, experienced deputy head who has been responsible for many years for pastoral care in a school, rarely needs nowadays to talk through proposed solutions with his head as appraiser. The head can show trust and confidence by leaving John to operate increasingly on his own. Because John knows his job and is keen to get on and do it, he appreciates the withdrawal of the head's supportive behaviour. It strengthens their relationship rather than weakens it. The risk is that the solutions John identifies and implements will not fall within parameters acceptable to the school. The head needs to know John well through a long period of managing in the participative style, must be available to talk with John if he wants a reversion to that style on a particular issue, but must otherwise take the risk. The appraising school does all it can to minimize risk but is willing to take it. Developing people is a risky business but it creates the climate in which people can grow.

A further risk the appraiser runs in adopting true delegation as a style of management is the chance of a mistake. Mistakes can, of course, be made within any style of management, and mistakes are the cost of creative solutions. If fear of making mistakes dominates our actions we fail to look for new solutions to problems. But with delegation there is one further danger: that the mistake will be covered up by the teacher and may go undetected until the situation becomes much worse. If our diagnosis of maturity is sound, the teacher will disclose or act on the mistake while it is easier to correct; discussion of it could prove a learning experience for others. The attitude which causes a teacher to cover up a mistake rather than acknowledge it reflects badly on the teacher and appraiser relationship and leaves the error to fester within the school system. The organization has to develop a positive attitude towards mistakes or it will limit the confidence of staff to be managed under the delegation style. The appraising school has a positive attitude to reporting mistakes and sees them as opportunities to learn.

A final point to be made about this style of management is that delegation does not mean abdication. The three key implications in delegation are:

1. Authority to decide and act. This implies agreement on the purpose of the task, giving the teacher room to achieve it in the way he or she operates best. It will also mean informing others that the teacher now has increased authority.
2. Area of responsibility. Be sure that the teacher is clear in which aspects of work he or she has authority. It may be that it is in the whole of the basic task, targets and other specific responsibilities, but possibly some of the targets and responsibilities should remain in participative style. There could perhaps be one unfamiliar responsibility which still requires the sell or even the tell style.
3. Accountability. Reviews need to take place at agreed intervals. Without reviews delegation becomes abdication; with too frequent reviews the appraiser shows a lack of trust. For most tasks the regular yearly or half-yearly appraisal interview is ideal, but be available for consultation if the teacher needs it. Agree on assessment criteria to ensure the teacher knows how to judge success.

The aim of flexible management is not only to get the job done but to develop the confidence, skill, knowledge and attitude of all staff. In this way fewer aspects of their work will need to be managed in the tell and sell styles; increasingly, as mature, confident and assertive colleagues, they will be managed through participation and delegation. The effective appraiser must ask, 'Have I been adjusting my style and so developing my staff?' Using a style of management which is appropriate to the teacher and the situation is not two-faced or weak. It is the essential skill of appropriate management.

The appraising school knows that if it wants good staff it has either to appoint them from outside the school, probably on higher than average scales, or to develop its own. Developing your own staff is:

- Better for staff morale because staff feel valued.
- Better for staff morale because people are promoted to positions of influence and responsibility inside the school. Every promotion inside the school reinforces in the minds of staff the qualities which the appraising school wants to promote.
- Better for staff morale because more people are promoted out of the school. Every promotion to a post inside or outside the school encourages others to develop their own promotable qualities.
- Less expensive because less expensive staff are being developed to hold responsible positions at a younger age.
- Less expensive because fewer staff are allowed to stagnate in posts which hold high salaries; more feel capable of further challenges elsewhere.

The important role of positive feedback in developing staff will be presented in detail later in the book (see Chapter 31), but it is appropriate to remember its role which runs across all management styles. In the appraising school people who are appraisers use feedback as a management tool to develop both their relationship and the teacher's effectiveness. They praise good performance. Not the kind of praise that 'Old Mr Grace' gave on the TV sitcom *'Are You Being Served'*, when he inevitably told the store staff 'You've all done very well', without having the slightest idea what they had done. In the appraising school praise is

- specific,
- descriptive and,
- reinforces behaviour for the future,

'Thank you for the way you dealt with that distressed pupil this morning, Francis. You have a great facility for good counselling.'

'Your administration really has improved since we spoke about it, Angela. Not a deadline missed in two terms. Keep it up.'

'I've never seen a better poetry lesson than you produced with your class today, Clive. That was an excellent device for helping students feel the emotion in the poem.'

Praise is like honey – great in spoonfuls intended specifically for you but sickening when poured over the whole team. Generic praise is a meaningless insult to the intelligence and performance of those over whom it is poured. Specific, descriptive feedback is hard to overdo. It helps to build a climate in school whereby people motivate themselves, seek their own self-development and so help the school to achieve its targets.

Recent changes in management styles in schools

In 1983 I conducted small-scale research into the style most frequently used within schools to manage teachers. I found little evidence of delegation being used appropriately as a style. It was being widely used inappropriately in that some senior staff who believed they 'delegated' work to their colleagues were actually in the 'abdication' mode, never reviewing performance even informally with teachers. Nor was there much evidence in comprehensive schools of the tell mode, except in a few cases which were founded on a grammar school with a strong authoritarian leader. In general, there was a marked absence of a management relationship of any sort between teachers, who were widely assumed to have the right as professionals to proceed along their own self-determined road, and the school, which felt obliged to rationalize what its staff were doing. It was less of a style of management towards organizational goals thhn a personalized support service towards unco-ordinated individual targets.

A similar small-scale survey in 1990 revealed how styles had changed. The most commonly used style in schools was overwhelmingly the sell style. Discussion with the senior and middle managers in the survey confirmed that they felt this style was appropriate for three chief reasons:

1. Low prestige and salaries left many teachers *unwilling* to undertake tasks which they felt were not compulsory.
2. The pace of educational change diminished the value of their current knowledge and experience, while poor dissemination of the changes left teachers *lacking knowledge* of what was required of them.
3. The lack of provision for training left teachers feeling that they were *lacking skills* in certain new performance areas.

Lack of time on the part of the appraiser and the teacher made it difficult to operate in the participative style. Diminished willingness, skill and experience on the part of the teacher made ineffective any style other than selling.

The aim in the appraising school is to develop teachers so that as many as possible can be managed in the styles of participation and delegation. The prerequisites for this are knowledge, skill, confidence and willingness; in other words:

- knowing what the job is,
- being able to do it,
- having the confidence to do it,
- being willing to do it.

As has been said not all teachers can be managed for all of the time in one style. However, the aim must be to move to a higher level the expertise and orientation of as many aspects as possible of teachers' work; in this way styles that are less concerned with task direction can be used effectively.

10
POOR PERFORMANCE

Setting the preconditions for tackling poor performance

In the appraising relationship poor performance is confronted and a joint resolution sought. It is never glossed over or handled arbitrarily. Poor performance can sometimes be tracked back to inappropriate selection or to ineffective induction. Since we have examined those two features of the appraising school, let us assume that the fault lies in neither. The appraising school has made it clear that it is interested in and values people but it only appraises performance. The appraiser is helped in his or her approach to poor performance by some of the key features of the appraising school, especially

- A defined level of performance in the basic task. This removes one cause of apparent poor performance: disagreement about what has to be done and to what standard. Both teacher and appraiser have an early warning system that something is going wrong when performance in the basic task falls below the clearly defined and understood standard.
- An appraiser who is close to the day-to-day action of the teacher, is *responsible* for the performance of the teacher and leads a team to which the teacher belongs.
- A day-to-day relationship in which the willingness to give and take feedback is strong. The teacher expects to be part of the problem identifying and problem-solving mechanisms. The appraiser expects to make the teacher aware immediately and specifically when something seems wrong and wants the teacher to explain the facts as he or she sees them.
- A target-setting system to develop future performance.

These features mean that the teacher and the appraiser

- know what good performance looks like;
- accept that the appraiser as well as the teacher have a responsibility for guaranteeing the quality of that performance;
- expect ongoing feedback on, and discussion of, performance;
- use agreed targets to maintain, improve or develop that performance.

Confronting poor performance

When an appraiser has an indication of poor performance, the first action is to share it with the poor performer. Never save it for an approaching appraisal interview. The teacher has to be certain that the appraiser never holds on to information about performance – either good or bad – but will always share it with the teacher at the earliest possible moment. Unshared, retained information soon becomes at best a surprise weapon for the appraisal interview and at worst a secret dossier on teacher performance.

Teachers, like most professionals work, without close supervision so allowing poor performance to be detected less in the action than in the result. Typical of the form this result might take in indicating possible poor performance from the teacher is such collated feedback as:

- pupil assessments which fall far below expectation;
- letters from parents complaining about the lack of marking of homework;
- a rapidly rising number of pupil detentions or other punishments;
- evidence of deteriorating relationships and conflict with colleagues;
- telephone calls from governors, passing on their received objections to an aspect of teacher performance;
- external examination results which fall well below forecasts;
- parents dissatisfied with the quality of reports on their children;
- colleagues complain that the teacher takes from the stock of pooled teaching materials and never contributes;
- disorder and chaos in pastoral programmed tutorial sessions;
- repeated failure to attend departmental team meetings.

Appraisers identifying such possible problems of poor performance will need to be able to

- identify and describe the aspect of performance which is not satisfactory. Is it lateness, absenteeism, quality of assessments, frequency of marking, relationships with classes or colleagues, or ill-advised decisions?

- give instances or examples of this behaviour, showing how the appraiser came to know about them.
- explain how the behaviour affects the pupils, the department or the school.

Will teachers hide poor performance?

A teacher may try to hide poor performance because he or she has not been able to perform the task due to a lack of skill, expertise, knowledge or perhaps time. If so, we have created an unproductive relationship between the teacher and appraiser, since it is the essence of the appraising relationship that the shortfall be discussed and tackled, not hidden. By stressing that performance appraisal exists to improve performance we will encourage open, participative discussion of shortfall. It is worth remembering, however, that one of the dangers of linking merit pay with performance of the basic task is that teachers will tend to hide weaknesses in performance rather than discuss them. This makes detection of the cause of poor performance more difficult and its correction more complex.

It is also possible that the teacher hides poor performance not because he or she is unable to perform better, but because of an unwillingness to do so.

Causes of poor performance

Lack of knowledge or skill

To help us understand how the appraising school handles poor performance we need to think again about the appraising relationship. That relationship manifests itself in one of four styles – tell, sell, participation or delegation. Earlier we reserved tell and sell for teachers who lacked the knowledge or skill to perform a certain part of their task, or for that rare group of teachers who were unwilling to perform. The former group would welcome telling and selling (or coaching) in the job because, if done sensitively and successfully, they would remove the cause of the teachers' poor performance. In fact, sometimes one might wonder at the awareness of an appraiser who puts a teacher into any situation without the necessary knowledge or skill to perform it.

In many cases of poor performance, the appraiser may search for the cause in the teacher's lack of information, specific ability or skill. Lack of knowledge might be resolved by making sure the teacher knows where to turn for information. Subject knowledge might be provided by the appraiser or the departmental team, or maybe distance learning or an off-site course is the answer. The acquisition of missing skills may be a more difficult task. Skills need tuition, practice, feedback and more practice. The most cost-effective as well as the most tuition-effective solution may be on-the-job training within the department, especially if a departmental colleague will accept as a target the skills training of the teacher.

Too much pressure

Stress is a frequent cause of poor performance among teachers and may have a variety of sources:

1. Community induced stress
The national changes in the education system with which schools found it hard to cope in the late 1980s and early 1990s induced stress among many teachers. Poor planning of the changes, failure to present them as a co-ordinated package, the rapid pace of the changes, lack of training and resources all made it hard for teachers to maintain a standard with which they were satisfied – in itself a further cause of stress. The stress manifested itself through both of the two classic responses to concern – flight (sickness and absenteeism) and fight (refusal to take on extra tasks, insistence on training for even minor changes of role, quarrelsome attitude to those implementing change, reluctance to take initiatives or decisions).

2. School-induced stress
The school itself can induce stress by its management. Springing surprises, delaying the implementation of changes which staff know are scheduled, unfair criticism – all these and more are the normal diet in some organizations.

3. Domestic stress
The stress which manifests itself in school may have its roots at home in family conflict, bereavement, alcoholism or some other personal source.

Solutions to the various forms of stress are more difficult to prescribe. Community-induced stress would be eased for the whole profession if those who represent teachers nationally could convince the government of the benefits of managed change – managed, that is, at a pace which those implementing it can handle and still perform at a satisfactory level. Take heart from the fact that such major changes as those in the Education Reform Act 1988 are cyclical. School-induced stress will be reduced as the appraising relationship develops; feedback to appraisers will help them to improve their management skills in ways not open to schools where feedback is avoided. Joint critique of progress will become routine. Home-induced stress may well need professional counselling and medical help with school support.

Lack of motivation

According to Maslow (1954) the highest form of personal need is the need to keep meeting new challenges, to improve oneself, to be the best that one can be. This need ranks above the need for status and the esteem and respect of others, which in turn ranks above the need for companionship, friendship and team spirit. Satisfaction for none of these needs can be bought. They are satisfied, according to the research of Herzberg (1966), by motivators such as recognition, responsibility, challenge and a job one enjoys. Teachers in the appraising school will not find these challenges missing from their professional lives, where there is a constant search to provide this form of motivation. But Herzberg supports our experience and common sense with another of his contentions: working conditions, super-vision and school administration, which he calls 'hygiene factors', need to be at such a level that they do not actively cause dissatisfaction, but im-proving these hygiene factors alone will not improve motivation. A person who needs a challenge needs a challenge, not just a new office!

But motivation is a joint responsibility. No teacher can sensibly say to the appraiser 'Here I am. Now motivate me.' That door is locked from the inside, believes Robert Townsend (1970). My good friend David Warwick (1984), in a book on motivation written for the Industrial Society, explains how he has found it useful to use Maslow's hierarchy of needs as the basis of a discussion with a teacher on motivation. He says:

> Convert Maslow's pyramid into a ziggurat. Now, begin the interview/conversation at the apex. In general terms, how does the individual feel that he or she is 'unfulfilled' (in whatever terms this is being expressed)? It is unlikely that the solution will be found in this general area, although you may discover precisely what 'being fulfilled' means to that individual. So, again in general conversation you come down a step in the imaginary ziggurat and consider the next level. The interview proceeds until, by careful yet friendly probing, you reach the true source of the discontent.'

In reality, the appraiser will have much greater influence in creating the conditions – the challenge, the responsibility, the development opportunity – in which the teacher self-motivates. Motivating is issuing an invitation. But I am with Robert Townsend in believing that that door is locked from the inside. It is probably impossible to motivate someone who does not want to be motivated.

Low pay

Maslow (1954) identifies the basic motivators as the physiological and safety needs such as food, shelter (or money to cover the mortgage), transport, etc., most of which can be satisfied by money. How many of us noticed how difficult it is in periods when teachers' salaries are in a trough, to motivate through challenges, team spirit and responsibility? Maslow claimed that these 'lower order' needs have to be satisfied first; that there is a hierarchy of needs. In practical terms I found that staff who are badly underpaid are too busy to bother with higher order motivators inside the school – they are busy finding ways to meet Maslow's basic needs by increasing their earnings from non-school work. Without reference to Maslow's theories, my staff performed the basic task and then turned their attention to an impressive array of part-time jobs.

The lesson on low pay will be quickly learned by LMS schools. Once teachers believe they are receiving a 'reasonable wage', it will be open to appraisers to draw the best from their teachers. When wages are considered unreasonably low, the financial saving in no way compensates for a poorly motivated staff.

Illness

The appraising relationship is one in which people do care about each other and want to help. The appraiser is aware that in most organizations there are people at work with varying degrees of illness, ranging from those who really should be at home and are not, to those who shouldn't be and are. The appraiser can foresee such categories as:

- those who are ill but are willing and able to carry their illness without it impinging on performance;
- those who are ill and can continue in post with support from the appraiser and the team;
- those who are ill and adjust the basic task, cutting corners in ways which are hard to detect in the short term;
- those who feign illness and use that as an excuse to produce a poor performance.

The appraising school is willing to give support to its teachers at any time, but especially at times of illness. For practical reasons it may be difficult to give support for long periods, though I have allowed teachers to set as a target the support of a colleague for a term or more. The appraiser confronts malingering, is willing to discuss problems, jointly resolve them and offer support, but not to tolerate laziness. Peer pressure, direct confrontation from the appraiser and insistence on the teacher seeking the opinion of a school-nominated medical practitioner are all considered fair means.

The working environment

Frederick Herzberg's research indicates the role of the working environment in good performance. Herzberg (1966) identifies factors which he calls 'dissatisfiers' – poor working conditions, bad administration and organization, poor communication, frustrating policies, etc. The least a top management team can do is to create the conditions in which teachers can teach by building lean, effective systems to support the real business of education which teachers carry out. Herzberg claims that rectifying such factors as these do not motivate people to work hard, but their existence does have a negative effect by making people dissatisfied and so encouraging poor performance.

Bad management

Much poor performance is the result of being badly managed over time by appraisers who believe their teachers are not capable of significant development and growth, who allow teachers to feel alone in an organization, who see things going wrong and do nothing about it, who cover up conflict. All these actions and hundreds like them have been the cause of teachers drifting into poor performance. Small-scale research of my own identifies the greatest 'turn-off' factors to be:

1. Not praising good performance. Don't take good performance for granted. If you want it to happen again, praise it now. 'The one-minute manager' has the phrase 'Catch people doing something right', and advocates that the minute following the 'catch' is spent in acknowledging and praising that action. In most organizations the managers spend more of their time trying to catch people doing something wrong and take the good performance far too much for granted. I can think now of a young teacher who took responsibility for a target in school, gave it everything she had for some weeks until it was completed and perfect, only to have no response whatsoever from her head of department. How many times does that have to happen before the teacher prefers not to take up a target at all? Morale in schools would be far higher if the people in them spent even half a minute acknowledging, praising or thanking people for good performance each time they saw it.

2. Managing in an inappropriate style. The style in which a teacher is managed has a powerful effect on the way he or she performs. This contention has been examined earlier in this book (see Chapter 9). If a teacher is managed in the tell or sell style when performing a task which should involve participation with the appraiser in decision-making and planning, then that teacher will change his or her orientation and attitude to match the way he or she is handled. The teacher may even leave a task undone until both appraiser and teacher can match the former's style and the latter's maturity.

3. Not delegating. One special feature of management in an inappropriate style is unwillingness to delegate. People see themselves as capable of significant growth and development, yet to a large extent the actualization of this is in the hands of the appraiser. Will the appraiser fail to delegate because:

- the appraiser is unwilling to let go of the task;
- the appraiser fears losing status if the teacher can more effectively perform a task;
- the appraiser fears change;
- the appraiser lacks confidence in his or her training of the teacher to perform the task;
- the appraiser enjoys the tasks which have become easy to him or her They require little thought or effort and the appraiser is loath to part with them.

The appraiser must be careful that lack of delegation does not hinder the development of a teacher to meet a challenge and gain achievement and recognition. Failure to develop teachers through delegation is not rare as a cause of poor performance.

Absence of management

Take the case of John Scrawn:

> John Scrawn is a graduate history teacher, aged 49, with 13 years' teaching experience, all in his present school. He is married with four children all over 20. He made a late entry at 36 into the profession from the Church. He is a knowledgeable teacher but ever since his none too successful probationary year, his head of department and head of house have carefully selected only the most malleable of pupils for his groups. He seems unaware of the poor reputation for discipline he has acquired. This is very evident in his dealing with a broader range of children, for example on duty or at lunch-time or when acting as a 'substitute'. His department head has found it easier to 'work round' John, sorting out only those problems which demand attention.

He is now pressing for promotion, and is uncharacteristically moody with senior colleagues at his lack of success. He is considering joining a course for aspiring heads of department, and has undertaken two counselling courses and a pastoral care course.

John is a caring tutor, much liked by his tutorial group, though they can pull the wool over his eyes when they wish to. He has no tutor programme organization, but it would be unfair to say that he did not know his tutor group well, or that his personal relationship with them was not good and pleasant.

John's administrative qualities are fair, though he tends to be lax over some matters such as keeping a pupil after school without notice of detention, failing to complete assessments on time and being late at meetings. He contributes well to the life of the school but never in a leading role. He is always willing to help anyone in distress, to be versatile for the sake of timetable construction and to join in any social activity be it choir, school visit, theatre visit or party. Teetotal, non-smoking but heavily overweight even for his six-foot frame, he feels he has been bypassed in life.

There may be no one in the country who has the exact combination of problems raised by this case study, though most teachers seem to recognize some characteristics from their own school in the situation. What are the problems?

- Poor use of the probationary year to identify weaknesses and begin a programme of improvement.
- Senior staff who prefer to 'work round' a staff problem than face a joint critique of progress with the teacher. Senior staff who seem not to have noticed that John is 'uncharacteristically moody', the cause of which might have been discussed with John as a classic sign of stress. Nor does there seem to have been much feedback on John's positive qualities, such as his personal relationships with individual pupils and staff.
- John's ineffective self appraisal, which leaves him apparently unaware of such fundamental problems as poor discipline, administration, lack of a tutor programme. Is he aware that responsibility lies with John himself, too, to contribute to his own development?
- A school which gives so little guidance on and preparation for promotion and spends its funds indiscriminately on an *ad hoc* range of courses.

Remember that poor performers are only good performers giving a poor performance: they are not bad people, a race apart from the rest of us. When you see a poor performer, think there, but for the grace of God go I.

It is not difficult to identify what should have happened if John's school had been an appraising school from the start. Honest relationships, support, a career development programme, etc. might have given us a vastly less depressing scenario to read. Which of us can say that at no time in our career were we less than competent at some aspect of our work or that we did not need the help and advice of a colleague or an appraiser? The real problem lies not in realizing what should have happened but in managing the situation in schools which have bottled up their frustrations and problems. As they begin to implement appraisal systems the initial uncorking could be as spectacular as opening a bottle of Dom Perignon, but much less pleasant. Bottling is for wine, not for problems. Never leave the teacher in a management vacuum; develop an appraising relationship.

11
DEALING WITH POOR PERFORMANCE

Discussing individual poor performance

- Talk privately. Keep the discussion informal, but make it clear what you want to discuss. Be prepared to provide specific details of where performance falls short and, if necessary, what the teacher can do to avoid the shortfall in the future.
- Use questioning skilfully to find out which factors create the conditions causing the poor performance. Most teachers are willing to talk about their points of pressure with someone who may be able to help.
- Use the jargon with which the teacher feels most at ease. Avoid wordiness; get to the point quickly when you respond.
- Listen. Resist the temptation to explain or defend until you have heard the full story. The teacher may want to talk through all aspects of the problem before you take some responding action.
- Show that you value the teacher's ideas and opinions. Be willing to explore them; clarify where you are unsure. They are likely to contain the solution.
- Many teachers are keenly sensitive to punishment and to being seen as incompetent. A subtle word or a reference to the consequences of continued poor performance may well have as much impact on performance as a formal reprimand.
- Be willing to accept anger. Find out afterwards what caused the anger and how this energy can be directed towards a solution.
- When a few possible solutions have been generated, discuss how one of them can be tried out for a set period.

If performance does not improve, there is the discipline interview which in seeking cause and solution can vary in emphasis from counselling to formal warning or dismissal. We examine that interview and its uses later in this Chapter (see page 80), but it forms part of the same advice on facing poor performance. No one in the appraising school will be left wondering if what they are doing is right or wrong. Their appraiser will be exchanging feedback with them as a natural part of a manager's job.

Giving a reprimand

We have just seen that the causes of poor performance are many and varied. Most of these causes intensify with time. Not all of the teachers who are bitter, resentful, unco-operative, unhelpful, quarrelsome or awkward began life in the school with those epithets as accurate descriptions of their performance. Nor are they necessarily true descriptions of their behaviour once they leave school and turn to their homes, hobbies, interests or community work.

The first step in tackling poor performance is, therefore, to face it. Make it a feature of the appraising relationship that you will give your teachers both positive and negative feedback whenever possible. In the case of poor performance, tell the teacher what you see going wrong. Describe the behaviour rather than evaluate it. Tell the teacher who has been late back to lessons after coffee and lunch breaks each day this week 'Jill, you have been late to lessons each day this week from Monday through till today, Thursday. This means your class disturbs other lessons and a colleague has to stop teaching to supervise them until you arrive.' Let Jill explain the facts as she sees them.

If the appraiser is not happy, say something like 'I feel you're letting us down when you are late. I need you to be here to take your class in at the start of the lesson. It's not like you to fall short on anything in the department. I value your experience and your reliability and it is not like you at all to set a bad example.'

I am surprised at the number of experienced senior staff in schools who will ask on courses how they should tell a colleague about an unsatisfactory performance. Many appraisers tend to leave it until they have built up enough frustration in themselves to deliver an angry outburst, usually to a group which includes the offender rather than to that teacher alone. Most of us have worked for the head who says to a staff meeting, 'I am very dissatisfied with the punctuality of staff to lessons in the school. We must improve on this as a school. We are becoming slack!' The reprimand is frustratingly inappropriate for most of the staff, has given the offender the feeling that everyone is doing it anyway and has not set it in the context of the teacher's overall contribution to the team. Face poor performance with the poor performer only – not wrapped in a message to the whole ship's company. We cannot afford to antagonize the innocent.

The discipline interview

Before we leave this question of poor performance let us look briefly at the discipline interview. This is not a handbook on employment legislation and so the current procedure, practice and recording for interviews leading to dismissal need to be checked and observed by employers. Having said that, the format for all discipline should follow similar lines. If they are handled well, most discipline interviews will never need to be repeated nor will they lead to dismissal.

A discipline interview checklist

1. Prepare the facts:
   - prepare evidence thoroughly showing exactly which aspect of performance is unsatisfactory, with accurately recorded and substantiated instances;
   - have available the facts on the performance standard required in the basic task and the facts on the actual performance;
   - prepare to establish the deviation between the two performances.
2. Prepare the location:
   - fix a time and date: never run a discipline interview 'on the spur of the moment', without proper preparation;
   - ensure you will not be interrupted. Never discipline a teacher in public or where you can be overheard;
   - set the room out so that the interviewee will feel he or she can explain and discuss, not merely listen to the verdict from the other side of the 'bench'.
3. Plan the structure of the interview and some questioning sequences, especially the open question which will encourage the teacher to start his or her explanation.

The style required in disciplinary interviews varies with the attitude of the teacher. Clearly, delegation is not appropriate as a style, since if it were the teacher would have drawn it to the appraiser's attention or eliminated the gap before this stage. The strategy is to move back through the styles until the appraiser finds one which is effective. Begin with participation. Can the teacher recognize the problem, discuss it, propose solutions? If so, participation would be the appropriate style. If not, move to the sell style. Can the appraiser show the teacher that there is a problem, demonstrate to the teacher the need to improve and convince the teacher of joint action which will close the breach? If so, then selling would be the appropriate style. If not, then telling is all the appraiser has left.

The tell style is the least likely to be effective because telling people they have a problem which they cannot see or accept is not a sound basis for building an improvement plan. People tend not to solve problems unless they believe they have them. However, such a style is appropriate for the person who refuses to perform the basic task. It is the style most likely to lead to dismissal. Dismissal is an absolute failure for the appraising school. It can shatter a teacher. When it has to be done, the teacher must have all the legal safeguards and the dismissal must be handled with compassion, respect and support.

In the interview

- Explain the purpose of the interview.
- Establish and agree on the facts:
  - use open questioning to try to get the teacher to present the facts to you;
  - if this does not work, present your prepared view of the performance, especially indicating the deviation between the required performance and the actual performance. Illustrate it with corroborated incidents or reminders of reprimands you have given the teacher on this issue. Be fair and accurate.
- Discuss the reasons for the deficient performance:
  - use open and closed questions to get to the root of the teacher's explanation of the facts. Are you sure it is still a discipline problem?
- Develop an improvement plan:
  - how will the teacher close the gap between the required performance and actual performance?
  - agree what will be done by the teacher, by you and by others;
  - agree on a target date by when performance will be satisfactory. Agree a review date.
- Now you know the facts, the explanation and the teacher's willingness to put matters right, issue a warning about future performance if you believe it to be necessary. Close the interview.
- Confirm in writing if you wish it to be a formal written warning. Record the fact that the interview took place.

Discipline interview conditions will vary between schools under LMS. Those responsible should ensure that they are fulfilling the appropriate conditions required by legislation and local regulations. For repeated and serious matters, having the teacher properly represented by a professional association adds to the efficacy of the interview. Professional associations do not defend bad practice in teachers and will always support a school which is as fair as the appraising school.

12
THE APPRAISING TEAM

Stages in team development

You cannot be an appraiser without a team to appraise. In the primary school the team may be the whole staff. In the secondary school, teachers work in departments or faculties. Their appraisers may form a middle management team, managed and appraised by the senior management group, who are also a team. The appraising school appraises not only individual performance and relationships but those of teams as well. How is a good team created? Clearly, the team is influenced by background factors such as the characteristics of members, whether their work gives them much opportunity to interact, their influence and status in the school, the history of the group as a team and, of course the influence on the group of its leader. Even with that in mind, there are common characteristics of team working which the team appraiser will want to employ, especially stages of team development, team member roles and team processes.

There are many analyses of the development of working groups and the alert appraiser will be aware of the stage that his or her own team has reached. I have called these steps in team development:

1. Stocktaking.
2. Welding.
3. Trial runs.
4. Harmony.
5. Long established.

1. Stocktaking

In the initial step, team members

- assess each other as 'the opposition';
- begin to identify a role for themselves in their own minds;
- feel the team is not sure of its purpose;
- fill the time with matters of working procedure;
- interact only a little, with a veneer of friendliness;
- exhibit little of their real feelings about being in the team;
- keep all eyes on the leader, when decisions are being made.

Any team which remains on this step is getting nothing from teamwork. It will retain the leader as a prescribing parent while team members, constrained by the need for security, become bitter and bored. The appraiser can move the team to the next step by using the listening skills, by encouraging interaction, by valuing the contribution of each member and by his or her own example as a team leader.

2. Welding

This is the team-forming step, in which members:

- voice their beliefs and thoughts;
- express their fears, feelings and reservations;
- form relationships based on improved understanding of members;
- bargain for and clarify their role in the team;
- become confident of the aim and purpose of the team;
- establish norms for ethos, relationships and decision-making;
- begin to feel that they belong to a team.

The appraiser should be sure that members are being treated fairly and consistently, and should encourage the group to evaluate and change the developing norms as appropriate. The appraiser should continue to encourage members to get to know each other, to respect each other's strengths and to express their own reservations. Building a team by glossing over disagreement will rebound at a later stage.

3. Trial runs

These form the basis of the cohesive, working team step in which members:

- build commitment to the team;
- undertake as a team ventures which are usually successful;

- are keen to review and willing to improve performance;
- interact well with each other;
- can handle any personal conflicts within the team;
- see to it that all members have their contribution recognized;
- avoid informal structures which are not similar to the formal.

The appraiser's team is beginning to work well. Difficulties may arise on occasions when the trial runs are not a success and when the openness of members becomes uncomfortable for some. Thus it is important to develop a willingness in the team to identify and resolve problems within the team.

4. Harmony

This is the mature, high-performance team step, in which members:

- effectively solve problems, make decisions and resolve conflict;
- clearly and precisely set high targets which they achieve;
- communicate openly with each other and trust each other;
- show a willingness to learn and grow;
- feel proud to belong to the team.

The appraiser now has an effective working team. The appraiser is now challenged to forestall any regression by making work challenging and interesting, providing opportunities for responsibility, growth and recognition. High-quality training and the involvement of the team in all decisions also help to maintain this stage.

5. Long established

This is the ultimate, self-generating step, in which members:

- have a high level of trust, honesty and ethics;
- are a creative, flexible, innovative group;
- behave in an open, creative and co-operative manner;
- are a regenerative group, never allowing their function to date;
- offer an established example to other teams in the school;
- show care, respect and support for each other;
- are proud of their continuous, high-quality achievement.

The appraiser now has a team which not only performs well at present and examines its own processes, but looks to develop itself for challenges it can see ahead. The appraiser may need to watch for the danger of pride turning to self-satisfaction, and for the team becoming so close knit that it becomes isolated within the organization.

If teams are to grow to become mature, the appraiser needs to be aware of such stages as these, however imprecise they may appear. The appraiser is often the greatest factor in ensuring that the team gets maximum benefit from each stage. For example, at early stages, the appraiser ensures that members 'become confident of the aims and purposes of the team' or that they 'can handle personal conflict within the team' or sees to it that 'all members have their contribution recognized'. Without this, a team will never reach its full potential.

Positive and negative features of team operation

In the companies where I have carried out consultancy work, the most widely used work on team-role analysis in training is that of R. Meredith Belbin (1981). Analyses based on his work identify eight team roles:

- Innovator
- Resource investigator
- Chair
- Shaper
- Evaluator
- Team worker
- Organizer
- Finisher.

Belbin defines each of the roles and helps the individual to identify his or her preferred role. This work is thoroughly recommended to those unfamiliar with it.

Another way of examining team roles is to identify the positive and negative features that are necessary for successful team operation. A team appraiser should be aware of such features in order to give feedback on group development.

The positive features

1. Leading and guiding the team to work together effectively. Maximizing the abilities of the team, making sure the group has clearly defined its problem, its responsibilities and its priorities. Concerned very much with the management of process but also with the clarification of content.

2. Keeping the group working to the agreed plan Preventing deviation from the task and ensuring that it is completed on time. Concerned very much with meeting agreed priorities and deadlines.
3. Maintaining team harmony. Oiling the wheels of the team machine with warmth, friendliness, humour, encouragement; keeping a sense of proportion about emotional differences, helping communication to flow.
4. Checking the perception of the team. Clarifying what people are saying and meaning, making sure the team understands and agrees. Summarizing progress and results so that the team is always aware of what it is doing.
5. Bringing issues out into the open. Keeping the organizational climate healthy by watching for occasions when people are hiding their real feelings on issues and professionally confronting them so that a joint resolution can be sought.
6. Attacking problems, not people. Seeing the problems with a plan and identifying ways in which these can be solved. Listening, exploring alternatives, encouraging the team to work out the best solution.
7. Supporting and contributing to the work of the group. Offering ideas, enhancing the contributions of others, getting involved in the work, encouraging others by example.
8. Brain-storming and lateral thinking. Preventing a team continually thinking along the same lines, questioning values, offering alternatives.

These different behaviours need to be present in an effective team. They are not intended to represent stereotyped individuals on an eight-person team. They represent qualities or features in a team, any number of which could be present as natural attributes of any team member. It is also possible for a team member to assume a particular feature for the sake of effective team operation. For example, if no one in the team naturally likes checking team perception and summarizing progress, a team member might consciously develop that skill so that the team is always aware of what it is doing.

Another use of this analysis of team features is for team members to identify negative, unhelpful features of team operation. Having identified them they are less likely to adopt them. It is recommended that any negative features are identified by the group themselves and that, in order to avoid the appearance of a vendetta, this is done before any group member has markedly adopted one or more of the features. The appraiser should watch, too, that the analysis is not being called into play at the first hint of negative behaviour, which the team member might quickly correct himself or herself. With these provisos, the appraiser can use team identification of negative features in a positive and constructive way.

The negative features

1. Dominating. Forcing ideas, monopolizing team time, intimidating others, a 'know it all' attitude, making decisions ahead of team agreement and generally acting autocratically.
2. Manipulating. Getting one's own way by looking hurt, dropping hints, flirting, saying one thing and meaning another and generally acting in an indirect and deceptive way.
3. Digressing. Time wasting, telling irrelevant stories, bringing in useless information, getting off the subject, starting splinter-group conversations or not being present for part of a meeting. Generally diverting the team from its activities.
4. Sniping. Wet blanketing by continually shooting down ideas, saying things won't work, being over-critical and judgemental. General attitude of stagnation and despair.
5. Assuming. Drawing conclusions on little evidence, replying before having understood the facts, presuming things about ideas and people without confirming them.
6. Withdrawing. Sulking, sighing, looking bored, being silent for long periods and not co-operating. General attitude of uninterest in the affairs of the team.

The role of a team leader, in addition to achieving the task and meeting the needs of the individuals in the team, is to develop team cohesion and mutual support. Essential to this latter function is an awareness of those factors which positively and negatively affect team working.

13
TEAM DECISION-MAKING

Why consult the team?

The chief team process of which the appraiser needs to be aware is team decision-making. The steps in decision-making are simple to describe, but difficult to deliver. They are:

- define the problem, its effect and dimensions;
- identify as wide a range of solutions as possible;
- decide on one of the solutions on the basis of one of the following;
  - the solution which gives the best result if the best happened,
  - the solution which gives the best result if the worst happened,
  - the opportunity cost of the rejected solutions;
- implement the decision.

In any organization, including the appraising school, some decisions will be taken by the senior management team and some passed to middle management teams to make. Few decisions which have any significant impact on the school are appropriately taken alone by any individual in the appraising school. The factors which make it necessary to work with the team for at least some part of the decision-making process are:

- The need for information. Much of the operation of a school has become so complex and specialized that the leader cannot define what the problem is nor examine a full range of possible solutions without the facts, opinions and judgements of members of his or her team. The leader may not even be aware of what information is missing from a situation, may not be sure where or how to obtain it, may not be sure how to analyse it.

- The need for commitment. Sometimes the team is willing to commit itself to any decision made by the leader. The team does not want to participate in the decision made and is happy to abide by whatever the leader decides. Maybe the team members believe the leader has greatest expertise, or that it is the leader's prerogative and duty to decide. Much more commonly, however, the school needs the commitment and enthusiastic support of the team for the decision. In making any decision which requires the commitment of others, the commitment and support of the team are more likely to be obtained if the team has been involved in the decision-making process.

Where should the decision be made?

As equally important as how decisions are made, is where they are made and who participates in their making.

The relevance of the decision

In the appraising school, appraisers expect to consult their teams about decisions, but not to waste teacher time on decisions which have no importance for the team or its working. Situations which teachers feel have little impact on them, and where they do not feel strongly about the outcome, are not passed to the team. It is appropriate for such decisions to be made quickly by the appraiser, so that there is no undue delay in decision-making which might set a precedent for indecision in the future. Conversely, the more important the decision is to the team, the more likely the manager in the appraising school is to be participative He or she expects that this involvement will add to the quality of the analysis, the decision and to the commitment to it.

The appraising school does not follow the practice of those establishments where participative methods are used only for decisions which have no impact on the school, while those situations which more strongly affect the individual, the team or the school are taken autocratically. Such action, in the long term, erodes staff maturity rather than develops it. In the short term, it can sometimes be justified by the nature of the change taking place, by time pressure or by the need to train staff to make 'soft' decisions before passing them those decisions requiring a high-quality analysis. Assessing staff effectiveness and maturity as low and using the tell style is acceptable in certain situations; feigning to use participative methods to conceal the use of an authoritarian style is not. Haven't we all met the head who rejects the decision of a staff working party because it failed to come up with the decision he or she had already taken privately? By all means develop staff maturity by training staff in the skills of group decision-making and by increasing the importance of the decision they are asked to take. But be open with staff about the nature of the developmental process in which they are involved.

The expertise to make a decision

In all decision-making, the appraiser seeks the best decision that the organization can make; this often means going to the team to collect and collate relevant information. Frequently, in organizations as complex as schools, an appraiser is not merely taking advice on which alternative action to take, guided sometimes by the experience of similar situations faced in the past. More likely, the appraiser may not know the nature of the problem, its cause or its likely solution and may have no precedents to guide his or her thinking. Yet, some managers find it difficult to ask their team for information or expertise to help them make decisions, feeling that they will lose respect by asking. In fact, more respect is lost when the resulting autocratic decision is far from the best decision the school could have made. In an environment where the teacher's opinion seems not to matter, it is little wonder that maturity and effectiveness decline.

Winning commitment to the decision

For many decisions, the commitment of the team to the decision is vital. The appraiser is aware that this commitment is best obtained by encouraging the team to participate in the decision-making process. In the appraising school, the basic task has clearly stated standards of performance, and failure to meet these standards can legitimately be corrected. Though commitment to the activities of the basic task will ensure a more enthusiastic response from the teacher, a school can operate even if not all of its staff undertake the basic task with enthusiasm. Mere compliance will produce a performance which allows the school to function.

However, any targets set outside the standards of the basic task will require commitment because the appraising school has no authority to ensure their accomplishment. Participation and delegation are, therefore, again seen to be the target management styles of the appraising school. This is still not to say that teachers will want to, or should be involved in every decision which affects them. Sometimes, because of his or her special expertise, teachers expect the appraiser to make the decision. At other times, that expectation is rooted in a different power base – that of positional power – when teachers feel that the appraiser has the right and the duty to decide. Or it is rooted in information power – when they feel the appraiser is familiar with a greater range of background data to inform his or her thinking, and so should decide. Or the appraiser has had great success with resolving similar problems in the past and this has inspired teachers' confidence. But teachers in the appraising school expect to know that a decision is being made and to have an appropriate say in who takes it.

Shared aims

The high degree of involvement of teachers in decision-making in the appraising school emphasizes the importance of the appraiser staying close to his or her team and listening and talking to its members. To expect a team to analyse a school situation, put up alternatives and select their favoured one, only then to overrule their decision, destroys confidence and generates cynicism. Why might an appraiser overrule in such a way? Almost certainly because teachers have made a decision which the appraiser does not believe to be in the best interests of the school. How could this situation arise? Because the teachers and the appraiser have not been communicating and now do not have shared aims, mutual interest in a solution or at least complimentary interests. Consequently they have developed different viewpoints on the nature of the problem or its favoured solution. It is important to discover such differences as they occur, to use the day-to-day relationship to identify problems and agree on solutions. Unless there is congruence in the aims of teachers and appraiser and agreement on how those aims will be achieved, then not only will the appraising school find it difficult to share decision-making with staff, but some part of its teacher effort will be dissipated in unproductive conflict.

What should the appraising school do if a decision has to be reached in conditions where, in the absence of unanimity of aims between appraiser and teachers, there are not even complimentary interests? It is inappropriate in those conditions to give the power of decision-making to the team, or to indicate that the appraiser will accept and implement any result which the team may care to nominate It is also inappropriate to use some of the less acceptable power bases to press through the appraiser's decision–bases such as fear, coercion, bribery, promise of reward or threat of punishment. The approach in the appraising school is for the appraiser to acknowledge openly the lack of compatibility, make the decision in his or her view of the best interests of the organization and begin work on re-aligning the interests of teachers and the school.

Decision-making in a crisis

Although as the appraising school aims to create the best possible conditions for its own existence, crises arise from time to time. Typical examples of such crises are:

- sudden, adverse weather conditions when the students are at school;
- a serious accident or incident at school;
- sudden illness or resignation of a key member of staff;
- a staff strike;
- misconduct by a member of staff which hits the national press;
- a group of intruders enters the school premises;

The appraising school expects crises and does its utmost to predict the situation and to prepare its response. Routine risk times for student incidents, such as lunch-time or the end of a school day, are easily predicted and so can expect a a sound plan and good staff cover, but those risk situations are greatly increased at the end of a term. Since 'ends of term' are foreseeable, a plan to avoid crises or to move in quickly if a crisis begins must be the obvious strategy. Good administration will termly bring up the plan for amendment and for staff briefing; conscientious execution will do the utmost to avoid the crisis. Make the situation someone's responsibility and expect that person to stay in touch with the moods and feelings that ebb and flow in schools.

It is better to overplan for a possible but foreseeable crisis than to underplan, leaving much to chance or hope. 'We've got a sledgehammer ready to crack a nut,' my senior management would tell me as their head. But we all knew it was best to have that sledgehammer ready in case the predicted nut turned out to be a particularly nasty boulder. Make it a practice each time a crisis happens and is reviewed, to ask: 'Could we have foreseen the possibility of this event? If so, what could we have done to avoid it? How can we make sure it doesn't happen again?' This is especially necessary with crises initiated by students, since with student misbehaviour the old saying 'If it happens twice it's a tradition', has particular dangers for the repeated disturbance of the environment of schools.

Even if we concede that some schools make their own crises by lack of forethought, lack of consideration of human nature, lack of belief in the law of probability and of applied common sense, we can still expect crises in all schools. The recommended strategy for coping with such crises is:

1. The leader must behave calmly. Panic shown by the leader induces panic in others and diminishes confidence in any rescue he or she proposes. It is not possible to insist that the leader feels calm, only that a calculatedly

calm demeanour is adopted to encourage the confidence of others. Within the leader, however, the nature of the crisis is at least as likely to cause agitation and distress as in any colleague.

2. The leader must act swiftly to understand the nature of the situation. Asking the questions 'who, what, where, when, why and how will give the leader the skeleton of the situation. Premature action could worsen the situation unless the leader knows enough about the cause and the prognosis to be able to make an emergency plan.

3. Put together an emergency plan. Never imagine as a leader that you have to invent it alone; be willing to call on others or even to let them devise the whole plan if their expertise merits it. But always clarify who is the crisis manager. If the management of conflict is part of the crisis, use the following analysis of approaches to decide on which one the plan will be built:

   - Capitulate. Take no positive action, withdraw or leave to fate to decide what is to happen.
   - Paper over the cracks. Take no action to solve the real underlying issues, but push away the real conflict while pretending that it has been solved.
   - Fight. Tackle the conflict with a determination to win and to leave the other party as a clear loser.
   - Strike a bargain. Each side gains a little and concedes a little, but tend to live with the basic problem rather than resolve it.
   - Solve the problem. The appraising school uses this approach wherever possible, since both sides gain by solving the problem. Progress and development lie in this direction. Any other approach will be only a temporary shelving of the problem, or it will be solved with a bitterness which will do little for relationships in the future.

4. Brief the team who have to carry out the plan. It is highly likely, in a crisis situation, that those people who are devising the plan will be responsible for carrying it out. As they make their contribution to the plan they will be simultaneously providing a brief for themselves or for others present. If this happens it saves wasting time on a second-phase briefing. Some schools have a recognized 'crisis management team'; others use all or part of the senior management team. If an *ad hoc* team is formed, be sure to give them authority to take the action you require.

5. Nominate a focal point for crisis co-ordination. Expect the leader to be there all of the time. Any forays he or she makes elsewhere should be brief and covered at the co-ordinating centre by someone authorized to take action. Brief those taking action to get messages back to the leader at the hub, for co-ordination, maintenance or amendment.

6. Begin to take second-phase action:
   - provide planned cover for those involved in the crisis;
   - look for action not sufficiently urgent to be taken in the original plan of action, but important enough to be in the second phase;
   - identify tasks which are certainly not urgent and can be safely left to be handled later, regardless of their importance.
7. Review the crisis once normal conditions are restored, using the questions indicated above to reduce the possibility of the crisis being repeated.

Team briefing

In the appraising school people pride themselves on using lean, swift and regular communication. One of the most useful methods of communication which enhances the usual pattern of whole school and team meetings, is team briefing. Widely used in industrial and commercial companies, it serves a purpose seldom addressed regularly in schools. Team briefing is a drill which helps to keep teams informed of progress towards targets and of selected, relevant information on current issues in both the team and in the school as a whole. This team briefing, strongly and positively promoted by the Industrial Society, has the following key features:

- Face-to-face briefing. This removes many of the disadvantages of written circulars to staff, much of which is relevant to only some readers, is subject to misunderstanding, provides no evidence of receipt and gives no opportunity to question or clarify.
- Small teams (4–15 people). Many schools have regular morning briefings of the whole staff by the head, which leaves the school with the problem of ensuring full attendance and of publicizing information which is of interest and importance to all. Team briefing can provide information which is department specific, yet can relay key information of school-wide significance which can be given an appropriate departmental slant. The team is a sufficiently small group to ensure that absentees are brought up to date.
- Briefing by the team leader. This requirement puts pressure on the team leader to accept one of his or her key functions – informing his or her team. Careful thought, data, feedback and preparation will be quickly apparent as the team is briefed by the person responsible for its performance.
- Regular briefing experience of the system operating in schools leads to the conclusion that briefing meetings held every two weeks are ideal.

Daily or weekly briefings are frequently less well prepared and lead to trivial time filling when there is little but routine information to convey – this may in any case be better promulgated as a staff notice. Briefings at more than monthly intervals lack continuity and encourage *ad hoc* meetings to bridge the continuity gap. Team-briefing dates fixed in the annual calendar help to make them a powerful feature of the school communication system.

- Relevance. The team leader has the opportunity to introduce and to provide feedback on items which will be relevant to the team. In operation the pattern which most often develops is that the first third of a 20-minute meeting is taken up with the 'core brief' – those items in which the team leader has already been briefed by the head. The last two-thirds of the meeting are devoted to the 'local brief', which is prepared by the team leader. Clarification is to be encouraged, but debate is not. Team briefing does not take the place of traditional departmental meetings where policy can be debated and planning agreed. Team briefing is for feedback and for notification about events and items of already agreed policy. Team briefing is not for persuading, problem-solving or deciding; it is for informing, in as crisp, clear and concise a manner as possible.
- Monitoring. Monitor the system to make sure that it is working. Staff should be aware not only of events, actions and deadlines but also of the results of team action, its shortcomings, its successes and achievements. The system can be monitored by watching and talking with teams who are all aware of what they are doing, and of why and how well they are doing it.

The structure of team briefing

Team briefing is particularly simple since it is based on existing line management.

1. The senior management team bring to their meeting all the information they wish to disseminate to staff. They decide which items to disseminate through printed notices and other means, and which to include in the briefing they will be holding with all team leaders. This brief is called the 'core brief'.
2. One of the senior management team chairs the briefing of middle management team leaders, talks through the core brief with them and distributes copies of it. Each middle manager in turn then outlines the 'local brief' which he or she will be giving to the team.

3. The next meeting is of staff teams, usually based on academic departments but sometimes on pastoral units. The team leader presents both the core brief, interpreting its particular meaning for the department, and the local brief which he or she has prepared.
4. A further stage can be introduced when teachers brief their students, based on material the teachers wish to relay and on appropriate items from the core and local briefs which they have received.

Team briefing has much to commend it for the teacher, the team and the school.

- For the teacher, team briefing provides an opportunity to check arrangements, receive public praise for achievements and be fully informed for the fortnight ahead.
- For the team leader, team briefing is a time saver which enables the leader to rely on a regular fortnightly meeting with no other business than briefing the whole team on the one occasion.
- For the school, team briefing is a personal information system which strengthens team working and minimizes the harm which flows from long standing rumour by shortening its life.

14
NEGOTIATION AND PERSUASION

Negotiation: balancing the deal and the relationship

Two skills essential in the appraising school are negotiation and persuasion. These are the operating skills of the two most widely used management styles in the appraising school – the participative and the selling styles. Negotiation may be defined as 'conferring with a view to compromise or agreement'; it implies room to bargain and manoeuvre, it implies participation with both sides hoping to meet their needs as together they create the final agreement.

Persuasion is the art of getting others to accept your view; causing a person to believe that a thing is so or inducing a person into action. It is a technique which implies selling an existing proposition. Yet the two processes are bound up with each other. Both require listening to the needs of the other party and both require a persuasive presentation of one's own case. The negotiator has to persuade the other party to see, in as attractive form as possible, what he or she is being offered. Persuasion is an integral part of negotiating.

Negotiation within schools is most often undertaken with people with whom the negotiator expects to have a continuing, long-term relationship. It contrasts with the negotiation for the private sale of a second-hand car from a newspaper advertisement, when neither party expects to meet again and both have the substance of the deal as their main objective. School negotiation, therefore, has much in common with most negotiations which have two major concerns:

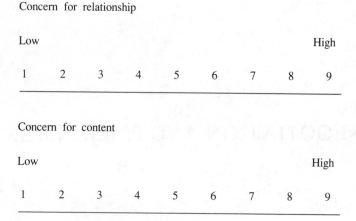

Figure 5 The two major concerns of school negotiation.

1. Concern for the relationship with the other party in this negotiation and in the future.
2. Concern to achieve the content of the negotiation.

Each concern may be expressed in the form of a continuum, indicating for each concern, the priority from high to low (see Figure 5). In any negotiation these concerns may either be equally balanced or one of the concerns may outweigh the other. If each continuum now becomes an axis, the relationship between the two concerns may be studied (see Figure 6). The extent to which each concern is present in the negotiator in any encounter allows us to describe his or her style of negotiating, since it is the extent of these concerns which governs the negotiator's actions.

A negotiator with style 1.1 is very low on concern either for the relationship with the other party or for the achievement of the deal. This negotiator takes the easiest deal that can be achieved and is unconcerned that people are upset that he or she can be seen doing this. The agreements this person achieves are a drain on school development, school ethos and staff spirit.

A negotiator with style 9.1 is high in concern for the content of the deal and low in concern for relationship. He or she is willing to use any means, including manipulation, threat and pressure, to achieve the best deal. He or she aims to achieve an efficient and effective organization, but people resent the fact that they are not respected; they tend not to trust this person and the lack of trust, understanding and honesty eventually harms the organization which the negotiator is aiming to develop.

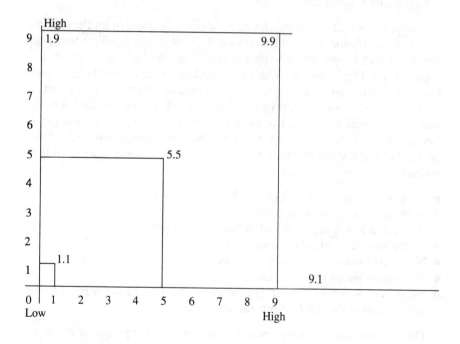

Concern for content

Figure 6 Negotiation style.

If the negotiator is overwhelmingly concerned to drive a hard bargain – to 'win' at any cost – and is only concerned with the substance of the deal, then the negotiation will be a hard and competitive one with features such as:

- Negotiator digs in to a fixed position and insists that the other side accepts it.
- Negotiator sees the other party as an adversary.
- One-sided gains are demanded as the price of agreement.
- Negotiator tries to win in a contest of will.
- Negotiator's bottom line is concealed and lied about.
- Negotiator finds ways to apply pressure and threat.
- Negotiator seeks to achieve the single answer – the one which gives the negotiator a 'good deal'.

A negotiator with a 1.9 negotiating style is low in concern for the content of a deal and high in concern for relationship. He or she is willing to accept the deal which keeps people happiest, even if the deal is a poor one for the organization. Deals tend not to be in accordance with the strategic plan of the organization and the school begins to lose direction. The criterion of keeping people happy begins to backfire on itself and people feel dissatisfied as they feel the school is aimless and drifting. If the negotiator is overwhelmingly concerned to preserve the relationship with the other party, the negotiation will be a soft, conceding one whose features might include:

- Concessions made easily to keep the relationship.
- Negotiator sees the other party as a 'friend'.
- One-sided losses are accepted to reach agreement.
- Negotiator surrenders in a contest of will.
- Negotiator discloses 'bottom line' easily.
- Negotiator yields to pressure.
- Negotiator searches for a single answer – the one the other person will accept so that the relationship can continue.

The 9.1 and the 1.9 summaries indicate the extreme ends of the continuum of relationship and of the continuum of the substance of the negotiation. In a professional negotiation involving the staff of a school it is rare that the negotiator's aim would be to act from either of these extreme positions. More likely would be the intention to balance relationship and content. Examples of such styles are:

1. A negotiator with a 5.5 negotiating style is moderately concerned for relationship and moderately concerned to achieve a good deal. In practice

this style often means aiming not for the best deal, but for a compromise deal consistent with minimizing any upset to relationships. This negotiator moves slowly; if he or she cared more about both the deal and the relationship with the other party there would be a greater emphasis on solving problems than on merely reaching agreement.

2. A negotiator with a 9.9. negotiating style is highly concerned with the content of the deal and equally highly concerned to preserve the relationship with the other party. Characteristics of the negotiation resulting from this style are:

- Negotiators see themselves as problem-solvers.
- Negotiators distinguish their attitude to people from their attitude to the problem; being hard on the problem does not make them hard on people.
- Negotiators invent options for mutual gain. They focus on interests, not on a fixed position for either side.
- Negotiators aim to reach a result based on fair and objective criteria, never allowing the negotiation to become a battle of wills.
- Negotiators have 'fair standards' as their bottom line.
- Negotiators yield to fair principle not to pressure; they reason and are open to reason.
- Negotiators develop multiple options and aim for a wise outcome.

Negotiators who wish to move towards this style of negotiating from a style which they find to be concerned too little with relationship and too much with achieving the best deal, will gain from developing some of the skills described in detail in this book, in particular

- active listening,
- giving feedback,
- creating a climate for disclosure,
- assertiveness.

Developing a 9.9 negotiating style from one which is felt to be concerned too little with achieving an appropriate deal and too much with relationships, requires practice in negotiating method. In particular, it requires

- preparation for the negotiation;
- questioning to establish the needs of the other party;
- drawing out, developing and presenting alternatives;
- persuasion and the selling of a point of view;
- closing a negotiation.

Persuasion – a key skill in negotiation

Much of what, in schools, is loosely termed 'negotiation' is in fact persuasion. It is persuasion because one person is trying to convince another to accept a decision or to act in a predetermined manner. Negotiation is a participative process when there is room to reach an agreement on the decision or action. If there is no room to manoeuvre and no opportunity for participation, then never pretend that there is. Teachers will rightly resent being invited to participate only to discover that what the other party had in mind was pure persuasion. Nevertheless, there is a role for persuasion in schools. Successful persuasion goes beyond mere compliance. It leaves the other party not only happy to accept your views and to act on them but also ready to persuade others to do so as well. A strategy for persuasion has three phases: preparation, conducting the persuasion and following up.

Preparation

1. Clarify in your own mind who has to be persuaded of what.
   - Are you sure they have to be convinced? What would be lost if they were not convinced but merely told of the decision?
   - Would mere compliance with a decision serve the purpose?
   - Is there really no room for negotiation?
   - What will happen if the teacher cannot be persuaded? Will the decision still stand?
   - Will the teacher be told to accept without being convinced? What will be the results of this?
2. Marshall all the facts and evidence you may need during the persuasion process.
   - People are seldom persuaded by being flooded with data, but have appropriate information at your fingertips ready to use.
3. Put yourself in the other person's position.
   - Talk to the other person. Use your questioning techniques to help you to understand.
   - Estimate what the other person has to lose or gain.
   - Practise expressing his or her opinions.
   - Empathize. Try to feel what the other person is feeling.
   - Show a genuine interest in the other person and in the effect of the change on him or her.
4. Prepare your arguments.
   - Anticipate objections.
   - Stress the gains and benefits.

Conducting the persuasion

1. Get the other person's attention and interest.
   - Tell the other person implicitly or explicitly, 'There's something in this for you'.
2. Begin with common ground.
   - Get him or her used to agreeing.
   - Aim to encourage a receptive attitude in the other person.
3. Listen to what the other person has to say.
   - Identify the other person's fears.
   - Show understanding of his or her needs: this will encourage the other person to try to understand your needs.
   - Never assume you have to keep on talking until the other person concedes.
4. Move slowly through your presentation.
   - Aim to overcome those fears which are obstacles.
   - Aim to get the other person contributing; leave room in what you say for his or her participation.
   - Aim to make it the other person's proposal as well as yours.
   - Leave the other person a way out from the opposition he or she has shown.
5. Positively sell the benefits.
   - Show your own belief and conviction.
   - Present the full beneficial effects from your listener's viewpoint.
   - Do not try to persuade him or her that there is absolutely no risk; put the proposition into a context where the risk seems acceptable.
   - In a group context invite the member who is convinced to explain to the one who is not – the 'persuader's helper.'
6. Avoid sandpapering.
   - Beware of arrogance, rudeness, scoring personal points, winning debating points, creating anger, scolding, springing a trap. They all make persuasion harder.
   - Treat the other person with respect; never make him or her look or feel foolish.
   - Never let your attitude say 'I know what's best for you better than you do'.
7. Maintain your credibility.
   - Accept your responsibilities. Never hide behind others ('I wouldn't ask you if it were left to me but the head wants me to ask you to do this').
   - Be honest; never deliberately mislead. You may need the other person's trust in future situations.

- Never misrepresent the other person's case, especially when relaying it to others.
8. Quit once agreement has been reached.
   - Be sure both parties are clear about what has been agreed.
   - Never spend time going back over each episode; replaying the tape can lead to irrelevant disagreements.

Following up

1. Take action based on what was agreed at the meeting.
   - Confirm in writing the substance of the agreement and the action to be taken if appropriate.

In the appraising school people openly try to persuade each other, regardless of their position in the hierarchy. People are not so passive that they are unwilling to tell others what they would like to happen, nor are they so aggressive that they do not see the need to respect the rights of others.

Effective persuasion depends on knowing well the abilities, needs and wants of the person to be persuaded. Such knowledge includes

- fears and hopes for the future;
- skills and knowledge which they have and those which they will need if the persuasion is successful;
- likes and dislikes;
- self-vision of the person to be persuaded.

Then present the proposal in terms of how it will satisfy that person's needs. Support this with a rationalization of the change in context as a logical move. In the appraising school there is a role for persuasion when one person has a sound proposition, believes in it and wants to persuade skilfully, so that the other person not only accepts the change, but acts on it with enthusiasm.

The negotiating process

A negotiation starts with both parties having a goal to achieve; if the needs of the two people in a negotiation are not compatible, there will be no negotiated agreement. Negotiating is not a matter of talking the other person into accepting your priorities; that is a *win/lose* situation In a negotiation you are aiming to show that by getting something which you want, the other person also gets something they want – that is, a *win/win* situation. The persuasion element in negotiation is in encouraging the other person to consider his or her needs from a new perspective, without insisting that those needs are wrong.

The three main stages in a negotiation are:

1. the preparation stage,
2. the dialogue stage,
3. the follow-up stage.

1. The preparation stage

- Identify the true subject of the negotiation:
  - be clear for your own benefit what you believe you are to negotiate about.
- Define your objectives:
  - be clear what you want to achieve at the end of the negotiation.
- Gather information:
  - follow the above advice on persuasion to ensure that you know the other person as well as possible and have persuasively adapted your proposal to suit his or her needs.
- Assess what room you and they have for manoeuvre:
  - each party has a 'most favoured position', which represents the best he or she hopes to achieve and a 'bottom line' which is the worst for which he or she will settle. Both parties have a range of positions they are willing to accept. The deal will be struck within that part of the range which overlaps with the range of the other person. Preparation means clarifying your own range and trying to predict the range of the other person.
- Plan your strategy and tactics:
  - a strategy is the plan for the negotiation; tactics are the moves made in pursuit of the strategy.

2. The dialogue stage

- The opening, which might include any of the following:
  - presentation of summary from each side which sets out their initial goals and feelings;
  - a review, from both parties, of the background leading to the negotiation;
  - the specific issues between the two people are defined.
- Discussion and argument:

- each person presses his or her perspective on the issue and questions the perspective of the other;
- opportunity for each party to present his or her proposition again, in a different way, to maintain movement in the negotiation.
- Bargaining:
  - people identify areas of common interest and adjust the position with which the negotiation began;
  - people exchange concessions, fall back and compromise.
- Closing and agreement:
  - both people agree on a single summary of how the newly agreed common interests will be actioned.

3. The follow-up stage

- Follow-up action:
  - the agreement is formally documented;
  - The agreement is implemented;
  - to improve professionalism the negotiation is reviewed for its successes and failures.

Deadlocked negotiation

Even in the appraising school, negotiations and discussions sometimes reach deadlock. Be certain that it is deadlock and not a temporary tactical pause while an offer is absorbed or considered. If it is clear that both parties have reached a position from which they feel they cannot budge, then some actions may prove helpful:

- Step back a pace from the immediate issue and look in perspective at the negotiation as a whole. This in itself may reduce tension. Then,
  - point out what has been achieved;
  - have a break or move the negotiations to another location;
  - recall what you have in common and why it is to everyone's advantage to reach an agreement;
  - indicate the dangers of not reaching an agreement;
  - identify and clarify which specific sticking points remain.
- Keep the discussion moving on a parallel track.
  - Ask questions to discover the emotion behind the other person's attitude, e.g. 'How do you feel about . . . ?'
  - Open discussions on another issue where success seems more likely.
  - Use the negotiator's two most useful words, 'What if . . .'. Without

obligation create new options within the framework of 'What if I did
. . . and you did . . . ?'

- See if you can get agreement in principle; leave the detail to another day.
- Lay out the possible alternative solutions and discuss under what conditions each of them would be acceptable.
- Ask questions about how the as yet unagreed solution should be implemented rather than about why it won't work.
- Ask questions which are close to the deadlocked issue but do not probe points which are becoming sensitive, e.g. asking the question 'Could you outline how we can judge the success of a history department?' to someone who does not want to implement a proposed change in the department. The other person then has the option of bringing it back to the proposed change or of talking in general terms.
- Last-ditch tactics – desperate measures!
  - Undercut. When negotiating with an unyielding head of a department, try taking the issue to a meeting of the whole departmental team.
  - Call in an ally or refer the other person to someone who can put your case differently.
  - Explain the action which you will have to take if there is no agreement.
  - End the negotiation and make the best of the consequences.

Negotiation and persuasion in the school situation

In what situations in school might teachers find themselves considering a negotiation?

- One of the parties faces a problem which the other can help to solve.
- Both parties face a common danger or threat.
- The feeling that one person can help the other one to gain, or that there can be mutual gain.
- One party wants to develop in the other a sense of need for a service or action that the first can offer.
- One party wants the other to provide a service or action.
- One party wants to extricate himself or herself from an existing relationship or agreement.

In many school situations several opportunities for management action occur in the same situation. Consider the following case from the viewpoint of a deputy headteacher and from that of a departmental head. Put yourself in the position of the deputy headteacher and consider which aspects comprise a *prima facie* case for persuasion, which for negotiation and which for the telling style or some other course of action.

The case considered from the viewpoint of the head of history

You are Edgar Morgan-Lewis, head of history at Priory School, a comprehensive school. You joined the school, at the age of 25, as head of classics in 1969 and transferred to become head of history in 1977 when the school became comprehensive. Traumatic as that was, you coped with the change and with the lowering of standards which came with admitting pupils who previously would have attended one of the two local secondary modern schools.

More recently, the change towards more 'empathetic' teaching and the new GCSE examinations have strained your skills and patience to the utmost. You believe that good history teaching is about constructing cogent debate around major economic, political and ethical issues of the past and, from them, learning for the future. Clear thinking, good essay writing and memory development are the chief skills which pupils acquire from your subject.

But the worst is yet to come. Now the sixth form and your A level work are to be infiltrated. History here at Priory School has consistently produced first-class results and a high percentage of university entrants. Now, one of your greatest professional pleasures is to be diluted and standards lowered so that 'core skills' can be introduced into A- and AS-level work in your department as soon as possible. For you it will mean a change of content and method, cross-curricular liaison with other departments and possibly a great deal of hassle from informed parents who foresee lower performance levels and lower grades. It all looks like volumes of extra work and a threat to the secure and respected position you have built for yourself.

Perhaps a strategy would be to delegate the changes to Rob Davies and Annette Woods, the two keen and able 25-year-olds who are the only other full-timers in the department, but this would almost certainly mean giving them the major portion of history teaching in the sixth form – which you are reluctant to do. Damage would be limited, if, out of the six core skills, you integrated communication and problem-solving into history courses and left to the other departments the rest, especially information technology, about which you know nothing and care even less! Also, it would be much more convenient for you if you did not have to begin any new teaching with the sixth form until the academic year after next. This would leave next year for the preparatory work and you would have no additional burdens in the current year.

This year is your pearl wedding anniversary and with your two daughters both at university you had promised your wife, who has never been robust in health, that you would take every opportunity during this year to have weekend breaks, short holidays, visit old friends and get to the theatre as often as possible. Perhaps you could negotiate a slow start to the changes or some concession to give you more free time in school. You know you would get no such concession from the head, an unsympathetic man with whom you have had to contend for years. Perhaps you can do better with his deputy. Pat Jones, only six months in post, is the deputy who has asked to meet you to discuss the strategic planning of the 16–18 curriculum.

The case considered from the viewpoint of the deputy head

You are Pat Jones, deputy head of Priory School, a comprehensive school. You joined the school six months ago to take responsibility for the curriculum and you see it as one of your key tasks to engineer the delivery of the 16–18 curriculum, especially the common-core entitlement, individual student action plans and shared INSET (in-service training). Shared INSET is already being pioneered, individual action planning is scheduled to grow naturally out of the existing records of achievement in years 4 and 5, but bringing the common core into A and AS levels is more of a problem. In general you feel quite pleased about progress with some of the core – modern language competence, numeracy and personal/study skills.

A key part of the strategy, however, is for communication and problem-solving and, if possible, information technology to be embedded in a range of subjects which includes history. The head of history is Edgar Morgan-Lewis, aged 46, who has a less than positive attitude to change. Edgar has been in the school since the late 1960s. You have had little to do with him, having met him only at middle management meetings, but you know he has made curricular changes only when they became absolutely essential. To be fair, however, he and the department are always thorough in all they undertake. History results at GCSE and at A level are the best in the area, as are university entrance figures through the department. Parents will be very sorry if this aspect of the school declines. There is no real possibility of the history department losing its post 16 work to the consortium, but Edgar does not know this and he might be galvanized into action if you hinted at it.

The two full-time staff in his department (Rob Davies and Annette Woods) tell you that they would quite like to pioneer new history courses, but as they said to you, 'Edgar does not encourage the destruction of his empire.' Since you control the timetable you could give Edgar a small amount of extra time in school and even more time if he would monitor one of the skills across the curriculum. You believe that no one can any longer use a department as an ivory tower; we all have to support, monitor and give feedback to each other.

Your TVEI (Technical Vocational Educational Initiative) contract requires you to plan the 16–18 curriculum in the current year and to begin teaching it in the new academic year. Your head will expect you to meet this deadline, though he does seem to respect your judgement in matters of curriculum delivery. Edgar really needs to begin now if the TVEI bargain is to be fulfilled. If all else fails you may well decide to tell him that curriculum change is part of the contract of a head of department and be prepared to supervise his implementation of the required changes. You have asked him to see you to discuss the strategic planning of the 16–18 curriculum.

A case study such as this emphasizes the need for appraisers not only to develop a range of basic interpersonal and managerial skills such as assertiveness, interviewing, communicating, negotiating and persuading, but also to make a priority of developing the appraising relationship. The skills and the relationship are best developed on the job.

PART III
STAFF DEVELOPMENT

15
IDENTIFYING AND PRIORITISING LEARNING NEEDS

Strategies for identifying the learning needs of a school

In recent years, at times when the term 'teacher appraisal' has been unpopular, I have helped many schools to set up what they prefer to call a 'staff development' system. The difference between the two, for some teachers, was that the former was 'boss initiated', giving priority to the needs of the school, and the latter was 'teacher initiated'. This implied for many that in a teacher-initiated staff development system teachers could select areas for self-development arbitrarily and completely divorced from job performance. I began to think of their attitude as the 'finishing school' approach to development, whereby people chose development activities in whatever they fancied for any reason which pleased them. Such approaches to development have no place in any school. In the appraising school, however, there is a strategy for identifying, prioritizing and meeting the learning needs of its teachers.

For a school the chief sources of information on learning needs are:

1. Retrospective sources (i.e. based on the evidence of past performance).
2. Prospective sources (i.e. based on planned or predicted performance).
3. Multi-directional sources (i.e. based on the search for quality in performance).
4. Client feedback.
5. Self-directed analysis of individual training needs.

Retrospective sources

Individual performance appraisal of the basic task

It is essential to have a clearly understood basic task for the teacher as well as a means of knowing when that task has been performed. Aim to identify the chief skills in each key result area of the basic task, and expect that teachers will be able to use these skills to work effectively in real work situations. Such skill analyses are useful in discussions between teacher and appraiser to identify relative strength in the competencies. The skill analysis is also useful in discussion between the teacher and any trainer or consultant with whose aid skills are being developed. If the skills are identified, much of the onus in proposing how the teacher can demonstrate relative strength in a particular skill is borne by the teacher. The analysis is also useful to confirm the purpose of the skill. For example, if one key result area of the basic task is to 'contribute to the efficient production of reports on students', some key skills might be:

- the management of time,
- personal organization,
- assessment and recording,
- report writing.

Many of the skills identified for one key result area will be useful in another, and teachers will be able to transfer their competencies to other tasks.

Feedback on the basic task of a teacher throughout the year, as summarized at the appraisal interview, identifies the quality of performance in each key result area. Any revealed personal need in the performance of the basic task must be every teacher's first learning requirement. Wherever possible, these learning needs translate automatically into development and training priorities.

Review of individual targets

Targets will be set by or with almost all teachers, with a few having targets set *for* them. Deficiencies revealed during the review process may indicate learning needs. However, since not all targets are essential to school operation, and may be merely desirable activities, more care has to be taken in translating learning needs identified in a review of targets automatically into development and training priorities.

Departmental review led by head of department

In addition to the appraisal of individual teacher performance, leaders of middle management teams will be reviewing team performance against planned objectives. The gap between planned performance and actual performance may identify a learning need for the department.

School annual review

The introduction of the school review, whereby the school examines its own performance, with the assistance, frequently, of an LEA team led by the school's general inspector, can also identify shortfalls. Being a holistic 'snapshot' view of the school it may not have the ongoing perspective of a continuous appraisal relationship. However, it has similar aims and may similarly identify priority needs resulting from current performance shortfall.

Prospective sources

School development plan

The development plan of the school will have established the changes in technology, growth and staffing requirements which are expected. Changes in internal policies or systems or in external factors such as government legislation will be reflected in the plan. The skill needs of the school for its future work can be abstracted from these data by using job analysis. Use job analysis for each new job identified to examine its component skills and tasks in order to produce a training specification which can be used either to prepare training programmes or for on-the-job training. Most schools appear to have at least reached the stage of constructing simple analyses as a guide to learning needs based on tasks × skills and tasks × people. The tasks are listed along one axis and the component skills along another, thus:

Task axis
- Buildings and maintenance
- Book-keeping and accountancy
- Marketing the school
- School administration
- Departmental budgeting
- Staff management
- Working with parents
- Evaluation and assessment of pupils

- Reporting to parents
- etc.

Skills axis
- Style management
- Delegation
- Team management
- Decision-making
- Negotiating
- Persuading
- Interviewing
- Budgeting
- etc.

In this way the chief skills in each task are readily identified and recorded and the future demand more easily assessed. The same form of analysis is frequently used to consider which job roles in the school need these particular skills, to record which are priorities and to keep abreast of training which is continuing, but this time the staff roles or names are on one axis and the skills are on the other. Gaps in the training programme readily stand out and so further learning needs are identified.

School succession planning

A company whose employees are comparable to those in a typical local education authority expects to enter into succession planning as part of its staff development. The small scale of schools, the relatively small number of middle management positions in a single school and their lack of interchangeability, all make succession planning rare. Local education authorities are inhibited by school autonomy from practising such planning. Succession planning, therefore, appears to occupy a very low position in the hierarchy of learning needs in schools. An elementary staffing plan would provide an analysis of the staff currently available and the movements of teachers which are likely during the period of the plan, for example due to resignations, retirements, redundancies, transfers, promotions and new entries. From these data and their comparison with the school development plan a training needs analysis can be compiled. The simplest aspect of the staffing plan to compile must be the age profile of the teaching force. In the event it is necessary to produce much more detailed information on the likely career progression of individuals in order to calculate what the training implications of staff movement might be.

Succession planning, where it can be practised, brings many other benefits to the school, for example:

- understudy cover for all key jobs;
- opportunity to show teachers that the school both knows and cares about them;
- opportunity to restructure temporarily;
- opportunity to reallocate graded posts temporarily;
- opportunity to promote internally or to bring in new blood to examine a problem;
- avoids the staleness which affects some long-serving staff;
- adds another dimension to the practice of delegation;
- the multiplier effect on others of the advancement of a colleague whom the school has groomed for promotion.

Individual development plans

Individual development plans can be used as:

- preparation for promotion;
- preparation to take on delegated tasks;
- stimulation and refreshment.

The peculiar structure of education when compared with major industrial companies makes individual development planning a haphazard, and patchy process. Development planning goes far beyond identifying the potential of individuals, helping them prepare for promotion and encouraging them along a career path. It includes challenging and stimulating all staff, including those who would not accept promotion, let alone seek it. Its essential prerequisite is a climate which encourages and expects people to seek and achieve development. In the education system there has been little such interest or action, even before schools were set into open competition with each other. Most top and middle management positions will be filled from outside the school; most teachers will secure their promotion by moving to another establishment. Staff who do not actively pursue their own development will not find their employers at all concerned. Local education authorities do not claim to help with career planning and career management. Competing schools are not prepared to develop staff so that other schools may be better managed.

There is a strong case, however, for rating these development needs more highly. A development programme brings to the school all the benefits of succession planning, but on a much wider scale, since it operates for all staff. An effective management development policy sets out to maintain and improve standards of managerial performance, while also supporting the supply of suitably trained and experienced staff to meet the future needs of the school.

Multi-directional sources

These sources are based on such meetings as:

Head's diagnostic team meeting

A meeting of the head, the senior staff and a consultant from outside the organization, could aim to make a periodic assessment of the effectiveness of the school, to look at the need for change and to find ways of improving the quality of the service the school provides. Such a meeting, which take place about twice a year, improves the chance of a timely change and publicizes within the school the attitude of regular self-examination and the search for quality. Its role is to generate ideas rather than to use its executive powers.

Middle management diagnostic team meeting

This meeting is run on similar lines to the above meeting, but is composed of the middle management team of heads of department, house or year. If the number of members is too great the meeting subdivides.

Department, house or year group diagnostic meeting

The departmental head and departmental staff meet to examine the performance of the department and, from the review, to assess learning needs. These needs will also be detected during the year, but at least on an annual basis the department reviews its own learning and training. Such meetings reinforce the philosophy of development as an expectation and an entitlement for all staff.

Day closure meeting for all staff

This meeting has been frequently used in schools in recent years since the inception of 'Baker days'. When related to staff learning needs this kind of meeting can take two forms. First, it can pool and collect information so that needs can be assessed. Second, it can make recommendations about how to meet needs. Clearly, it is most usefully managed in groups of five or six staff, usually in a cross-departmental mix. Staff must be rigorous and specific in their proposals, in itself a skill in which they may need to be trained or to be coached through practice. Like other such meetings in this series, it has the advantage of encouraging teachers towards self-observation, towards the need for change and towards the search for quality.

Headteacher review meeting with the head of each section in the school

This is a meeting for two people and as such can be more specific and more probing than the larger meetings described above. In any of the meetings described, it is sometimes beneficial to use a consultant from outside the school, who is well versed in consultancy techniques. Use either a professional consultant or a local general Inspector, where an LEA has encouraged the development of appropriate techniques among its inspectorate.

Client feedback

Client feedback may come from a range of sources including the governing body, parent associations, customer complaints and congratulations.

Parents

Trawling for parent feedback may be undertaken in such ways as these:

- Collated feedback from personal interviews with parents. Ensure that parents are given feedback on their children at formal reporting sessions in personal, private interviews. Usually this will take the form of a summary of progress from the personal tutor of each pupil. This exchange of information is a skilled exercise in itself, but it should have the imposed rule that no feedback from a parent will be left unanswered. If the tutor cannot resolve it, it will be passed to middle management to resolve. Pooling this feedback from parents, especially that which could not be quickly acted on, will give a client perspective on the school and will frequently indicate learning needs of staff, of which they may have been previously unaware.
- Field research techniques. These techniques aim to deal with the attitudes and behaviours of school clients towards the school, the factors underlying their preferences and their reactions to the school and its development. The principal techniques are:
  - Sampling. The collection of facts, opinions and attitudes from a representative number of clients. Useful for a speedy, low-cost reaction, even if the outcome has to be expressed in terms of probability.
  - Observation. Use all parental contact with the school to establish a pattern of parental reaction. Use especially large-scale, one-to-one interviews such as pupil reporting sessions (see page 120).

- Panels. A group of parents, comprising as representative a sample as can be obtained, serves as a barometer on all school matters over an extended period.
- Attitude scaling. Equally as useful to the school as behaviour studies are devices for assessing client attitude. Use either a continuum on which parents mark their reaction to a series of statements, or offer five categories of reaction to the statements, i.e. strongly agree, agree, uncertain, disagree, strongly disagree. Such techniques will not only give the school an insight into parental behaviour and attitudes, but will provide a major spin-off benefit through the identification of staff learning needs both for the present and for the future.

Pupil feedback

Pupil feedback can be obtained from teacher assessment, from colleague assessment or from the pupils themselves on certain issues, for example their view of the effectiveness of one approach as compared to another. Pupil performance also serves this purpose when interpreted with caution; a poor set of results could indicate that the topic had been taught in a confused manner.

A further form of pupil feedback is the pupil progress meeting, held by every department about three times per term to highlight pupils performing exceptionally well or badly relative to expectations about them. Pool this information for the whole school to discover whether a pupil is exceptional in one subject or in many, and to give the pastoral system advance warning of changes in performance. This system can also be used to pass on that advance warning to parents and to ensure that pupils do not remain for too long in a teaching group to which they are unsuited. Indirectly, this meeting also throws up learning and training needs of staff.

Self-directed analysis of individual training needs

Individual teachers may use a combination of means to assess their own learning needs:

- record and analyse daily activities;
- seek the observations and comments of colleagues;
- ask the departmental head or another manager to appraise a particular aspect of performance;
- consider likely career paths and identify the likely skills gap;
- compare performance with others who have superior skills;
- Keep a personal diary of management experiences.

Every teacher is responsible for understanding his or her own development needs. Performance appraisal does not aim to take away that responsibility. Certainly, the appraiser has an obligation to contribute to that understanding, but not to stifle the teacher's effort. Nor should the teacher stop at understanding the need; as we shall see Chapter 16 (see page 123) it is perfectly possible for a teacher to turn learning needs into a training programme and to manage his or her own development as part of daily working.

Prioritizing learning needs

Identifying the learning needs is one essential step in developing the appraising school. A second and equally important step is the prioritization of those needs, so that scarce training resources can be used effectively.

1. The first priority: shortfall in present performance

The first priority of learning need has to be drawn from any area of shortfall in the satisfactory performance of the essential task of a teacher. The first priority training need must be to close the gap between what a teacher can do and what the teacher must do in order to enable the organization to function.

2. The second priority: preparation for future performance

The second priority for learning needs has to be the provision of identified, appropriate skills for the planned future development of the school.

3. The third priority: other training which contributes to the planned development of the school

This training can be undertaken if it does not jeopardize, compromise or conflict with earlier priorities and if there are sufficient resources to meet that need. Where possible an attempt should be made to include such third-priority training within training being given at a higher priority level.

Schools would be well advised to publish a training and development policy statement. This would cover such aspects of policy as:

- The positive attitude of the school towards giving and receiving support, training and development; the expectation that managers would devote adequate time and attention to the personal development of their staffs and the expectation that teachers would expose, discuss and expect to solve problems as part of their personal development.

- The sources from which the training plan for the school are derived and learning and training needs established (as discussed above).
- The means by which priorities for training are decided, given the scarcity of resources.
- The role, status and resources allocated to self-managed, delegated and other on-the-job learning in the school.
- A recognition of the importance of the leadership style of managers in the 'on-the-job' learning of their teachers.
- How the costs of training are borne in the school.
- The circumstances and understanding under which time off from present work will be given.
- The extent of staff entitlement to training.
- The requirement to attend training, e.g. as part of the induction process, as a condition of appointment to a promoted post, etc.
- An acceptance of the importance of measuring the results of training.
- The responsibility for training and development in the school – usually a senior member of staff reporting directly to the head.

16
MEETING TRAINING NEEDS

How to plan self-directed training

Self-directed training can be planned as follows:

- Compile information on learning needs (see Chapter 15).
- Be aware of favoured learning styles (see Chapter 19).
- Consider where management learning and training opportunities exist in the school, and whether these can be complemented or supported by distance learning packages.
- Plan appropriate activities (e.g. to use a different style to manage a forthcoming team meeting, analyse the team briefing style of a role model, etc.)
- Build learning into normal daily working, e.g.
  - learn to try different behaviours to achieve familiar tasks;
  - ask others to provide feedback on your style and actions;
  - observe and analyse the management behaviour of others.
- Occasionally take on experiences in addition to the daily workload:
  - set up a self-directed project;
  - seek out and volunteer for additional responsibilities and experiences which fall in line with learning needs.
- Set realistic targets for the learning and training.
- Review achievement and, if necessary, the reasons for the shortfall.
- Ask colleagues for their advice, experience and coaching.
- Decide what additional experience is needed, either continuing in self-directed study or by discussing progress with an appraiser.

An example of self-managed training

Training in assertiveness

The importance of assertiveness in the appraising school has already been discussed (see page 26). The appraising school needs its teachers not only to know themselves and their needs, but to have a positive self-image. Its teachers are required to express their views and feelings in constructive ways without beating around the bush, to level with their colleagues and to expect their colleagues to be equally straight with them. Training in assertiveness can be self managed:

- Understand that people can be assertive in their own way. Your assertiveness should be open and straightforward, but it should also suit you, your situation and the person to whom you wish to express your needs.
- Practise selecting the occasions when you choose to assert yourself and when you choose not to do so. Mature people do not make a career out of persistent assertiveness.
- Expect to make mistakes in developing your assertiveness, mistakes of timing or of style. There is no need to feel guilty about this; it happens in practice sessions for all skills.
- Give your assertiveness authority by preparing your facts and your case.
- Identify the source of your anxiety if you feel stressed. Calm the anxiety if you can, but if not build it into your assertive statement: 'I'm really nervous about bringing this to your attention, but it is important to both of us that I do.'
- Let others know what you are doing if your assertiveness is likely to make them worried.
- Review your success at being assertive without being aggressive or passive. Do you feel better about yourself, feel less stressed, feel that you and your opinions matter? If so, you are also improving the quality of your contribution to the appraising school.

Planned management training within schools

Many senior staff are wary of becoming involved in the training of colleagues because of the role and style changes which they feel are involved. In fact, the role change to be made is one which is extracted from the basic style theory of the organization – the Hersey and Blanchard (1982) situational leadership model. This model advocates that the appraiser who manages a teacher who is low on knowledge or skill in an aspect of his or her work, uses the tell (instructional) or the sell (coaching) style with that teacher on that task. The model further encourages appraisers to use discussion, participation, support and delegation to carry forward the development of those teachers (see Table 2).

Table 2 Management style and training

Management Style	Development activity
Tell	Giving knowledge (lectures and instruction)
Sell	Giving skills (coaching)
Participate	Giving support (discussing problems)
Delegate	Giving freedom to operate (delegating)

There should be no more of a problem for the appraiser in changing style from manager to trainer or coach than in changing style for any other management reason. It is essential for the development of teachers within the appraising school that managers are able and willing to make that change and that they are trained as a basic skill to be able to do so. The importance of 'on-the-job' training cannot be over-emphasized.

Ensuring success in school-managed, on-the-job training

On-the-job training is the only real training. Other forms of development such as specialist reading, distance learning and off site courses all have their role. They may deepen understanding, but the nearest they ever come to the real situation is simulation. How can the senior staff of a school ensure in-school, on-the-job training?

. 1. Encourage an environment conducive to on-the-job learning. Encourage people to analyse their behaviour. Make it a regular school habit to review events, incidents and approaches, not only when they fail, as a form of inquest, but also when they succeed so that the same pattern can be repeated. Even successes can be improved if we know why they succeeded.

2. Provide and organize management learning opportunities. Many such opportunities do not need to be especially created but can be created from jobs which the school has to undertake. Offer the opportunity of the real task to someone whose acknowledged learning need is in that area. The teacher who is allowed the experience of planning and chairing a departmental meeting or of managing the department budget, the department head who investigates a cross-curricular issue in the school, the headteacher who allows the deputy to write and present a governors' report, are all providing learning and training opportunities if they are being appropriately offered and managed.

3. Offer feedback to teachers who undertake on-the-job training. Follow the guideline of effective delegation, giving proper preparation and spend time identifying performance criteria which will simplify the feedback process.

4. Offer to provide observable behaviour as a positive model. Much conscious or unconscious management learning goes on in schools as teachers see each other in action and learn from the model they observe. While I believe that most of my own personal management learning came from reversing and adapting the behaviour of negative role models and that this remains a worthwhile exercise, planned observation has the benefit of aiming to provide a positive model. Few heads would say to their deputies, 'Watch me handle this meeting badly!', whereas consciously demonstrating sound techniques benefits both the observer and the observed.

5. Offer coaching in an agreed area of development. Coaches sometimes pass on job knowledge and skills but are also in a position to influence the development of positive attitudes.

Senior school staff frequently find coaching difficult, especially if they have not learned to adapt their style to the situation. As has been said earlier (see page 124), coaching in itself is a style, closest to the selling style of the Hersey and Blanchard situational leadership model. Senior staff who operate for most of their time in their preferred style, for example the tell style of the authoritarian head, may face the teachers and themselves with the problem of coping with this new-style relationship. However, for most senior staff who see style flexibility as part of management growth, adopting a coaching style is not a problem. Time, in contrast, is almost always difficult to find. In the appraising school teachers give a high priority to the allocation of their time to developing each other. Even so, a time concession from the school's training allocation may be necessary during periods of coaching.

6. Undertake similar training themselves. Senior managers who cannot offer to their teachers coaching or support in a particular skill may wish to acquire that skill at the same time as their subordinate. An appraiser who wishes to refresh skills in the management of meetings might undertake the same off-site or distance learning experience as the teacher who is acquiring these skills for the first time. In putting the skills into practice in the school situation, teacher and appraiser share learning experiences, observe, criticize and coach each other.

7. Transform research or innovation into the form of projects; offer these as challenges to individuals or teams. This creates problem-based, action learning situations in which skills and techniques can be developed, practised, monitored and coached while at the same time pushing forward the development of the organization.

Using a mentor

Managers in schools, as elsewhere, are under pressure to produce results and to monitor their team. The time, and sometimes the appropriate expertise, which they feel they can allocate to developing others are limited. The existence of a mentor system allows other senior staff in school to help to advise, coach and develop certain specified teachers, thus sharing in the work of staff development.

Mentors take an active interest in, and have a commitment to, the career of a particular teacher. Mentors are sometimes used in schools to develop poorly performing teachers, and following an appraisal, the help of a mentor can be particularly appropriate in developing skills agreed to be deficient. But the process can be used with any member of staff, and another of its uses is in developing the most able teachers for promotion.

The mentor's chief function is as a coach. The problems of time and style for the manager who is expected to coach his own team have already been outlined. One solution to this problem is the use of a mentor to act as coach to some of the team on all development issues, or to all of the team on selected issues.

A second function for the mentor is to press forward the experiential learning of the teacher, helping to suggest or search out experiences that are relevant to the teacher's learning needs. The third function for the mentor is to use his or her experience of the school to help the teacher to appreciate the organizational culture. This does not mean indoctrination, but rather discussion, persuasion and guidance.

Getting the best from using a mentor

The use of a mentor system to support staff development include the following benefits:

- it provides a source of experience and information on career paths, development opportunities and promotion strategies for teachers;
- it forms part of the succession planning strategy of the school and of the education service;
- it develops the coaching skills of senior staff;
- it keeps senior staff in touch with the fundamental skills of the profession;
- it makes senior staff more aware of the views of teachers – their concerns, problems and frustrations;
- it provides teachers with the advice and support of an experienced senior manager;

- it lightens the load of departmental team leaders in the field of staff development;
- it offers a practical example of the participative and supportive ethos of the school.

The dangers to aim to avoid in the mentor system are:

- animosity from teachers who do not have a mentor;
- the misunderstanding of the scheme by staff and governors who may see it as one for 'pets and pests';
- the antagonism of middle managers if some of their staff have mentors elsewhere in the school. Let such managers decide whether they wish to handle the development of all staff in their department or whether they prefer to lighten the load through the mentor scheme;
- frustration if the mentor appears to be giving advice which conflicts with departmental policy. Mentors need to be sensitive to the need to keep departmental leaders in the picture.
- lack of coaching skill of mentors – train the mentors first.

In short, mentors should be professionally expert, be empathetic and have good interpersonal skills, especially in coaching, guidance, negotiating and counselling.

17
DELEGATION FOR DEVELOPMENT

Gains from delegation

Delegation is a frequently misunderstood term. In the context of this book, delegation is taken to mean the 'temporary transfer of a task from one employee to another for which the former retains responsibility'. In a broader context all tasks undertaken in school may be seen as the responsibility of the head, but those which are part of a permanent job description are not, in this present sense, delegated. Those tasks for which one teacher retains responsibility while another is given temporary authority to carry them out are considered to be delegated tasks. Delegation, therefore, in this sense, is a means of developing staff through training in a job distinct from their own. It can develop their ability to make decisions, to plan, to take action and to manage. Delegation has other strengths to commend it to those who manage others in schools:

- If you feel under pressure, find the days too short and have a heavy workload ahead, delegation can relieve you of routine and less critical tasks.
- If you never have time to plan and develop ways of improving and spend much of the day sorting out problems, delegation can free you for the more important work of planning, organizing and motivating.
- If, in your absence, things go wrong and no one can correct them as well as you can, delegation allows decisions to be taken at the point of implementation.

Powerful as these managerial contentions are, one of the most important reasons for delegation is its use as a motivator and developer of staff. If

Herzberg (1966) is correct in stressing the satisfying power of achievement, recognition, challenging work and responsibility, then one method of implementing this approach is through effective delegation. Any head who feels that the abilities of the staff are not broadening, that they are not being developed and used to the best effect, that staff are losing interest in the tasks they have carried out for years, must consider the principles of effective delegation.

The steps in delegation are few: select the work to be delegated and the teacher who will take it on, prepare the teacher to perform the task, find an appropriate method of support while that teacher does the job and, finally, review the work at agreed intervals. It is target-setting in another guise and is a strong feature of the appraising school.

Selecting the work

The most obvious work to delegate is the planning and management of regular events, routine supervision, routine decision-making and routine tasks. Consider also delegating the management of a change, the installation of a new system or the management of some truly important aspect of school development. Delegation of exciting new challenges and of important matters stimulates the feeling that people are entitled to growth and development in this organization. I have seen heads delegate many of the tasks they would love to retain themselves – innovations such as implementing the TVEI philosophy, setting up a team-briefing system or engineering certain aspects of curriculum change. For one reason or another, other heads manage them as delegated tasks because:

- the teacher concerned wanted and deserved a new delegated task;
- the teacher concerned could bring different skills to the task;
- the task was very likely to prove a critical career step for the teacher;
- the teacher would be better accepted by those involved in the change.

For some heads the tasks which they retain apart from the general management of others, are only those items which are left when their management team has picked those it would like to handle.

Selecting the teacher

Often the first step in delegation is not task selection, but teacher selection. Most teachers want to be developed in the profession, and heads who are sensitive to this actively seek out tasks to give to the teacher who is pressing to be developed in post. Other candidates to bear in mind as well as those who draw attention to their search for professional development are those who have to be encouraged in the confidence to seek extra responsibility, those who have an unfairly light workload and those who are becoming stale and uninterested in their post and may need the stimulus of a new challenge. Whichever comes first, the task or the teacher, aim to make them appropriate by careful matching of skills and skill development areas to the demands of the task.

Preparing for delegation

The step most frequently omitted in school delegation appears to be the preparation of the teacher for the task. Where it is undertaken, the most common form of preparation is an outline of the task, frequently without the key target-setting question 'How will I know when I've done it?' The chief forms of preparation which are suggested are:

1. Explanation in detail, with opportunity for questions, for confirmation that the teacher can handle the work and has an understanding of the criteria for judging success.
2. Demonstration of the task, with explanation, questioning, performance criteria and a trial run to ensure familiarity.
3. Full training, which can be at a formal, off-site course of instruction or a course of distance learning. When appropriate, working alongside a colleague and sharing in the task can add even more to the reality of the training. Though expensive in time, money or both, full training is an entitlement, not only for effective task performance, but also within the context of management development of the individual teacher.

Support for the teacher in delegation

The more usual forms of support for teachers undertaking delegated tasks are:

1. Support through supervision – watching the teacher perform, helping with difficulties and correcting when the need arises. Such a mode might be used when a teacher takes on a technically difficult task where a mistake might be costly if not swiftly detected and amended.
2. Support through checking. The leader does not wait for a call from the teacher but visits from time to time. This is suitable for a task where it is difficult for the teacher to be aware that a deviation or error has occurred.
3. Support by request. The teacher is not obliged to invite any support at all if he or she is happy with the progress of the task. This is suitable for

work where there is built-in feedback in case of error, which the teacher is trained to correct. If, however, a particular difficulty arises which the teacher cannot handle, the leader expects to be called in to help.

Reviewing the delegation

The features of good delegation are that the area of responsibility has been clearly defined, with its purpose, its limitations and its key result areas all agreed, as is the case with all effective target-setting. The teacher must be given authority to carry out the task and to take decisions on that authority within an agreed area. Others affected by this change of function need to be informed. The period of the delegation should be agreed, as should the review period.

Review the delegated task with all the review skills discussed in detail in this book. Give feedback which will not only improve the performance of the job but will encourage the teacher to continue with 'in-the-job' professional development.

18
TRAINING OFF THE JOB

What to avoid in off-the-job training

The term 'off-the-job training' is intended to include such activities as courses, lectures, seminars, workshops and other such planned training experiences. Though such experiences can be very valuable, they do not guarantee that the teacher can put into practice in the live situation, the skills and knowledge acquired 'off the job'. The weaknesses of these planned activities, some of which can be avoided, are:

1. They are designed to meet the needs of a group. Course members may find the experience comes close to meeting their need, but it will seldom be sufficiently personalized to meet the needs of all. However, the smaller the group of participants and the better known to the activity leader they can become, the more likely it is that individual needs will be met.
2. The tendency for providers to provide what they believe the participants need. This 'provider-initiated' activity is much on the decline from days when providers provided what they could most comfortably offer without reference to the intended participants. Even today, there is still much evidence of bulk buying: of the packaged course being fed, especially by institutions, to cohorts of managers from a large customer, such as an LEA.
3. The lack of selection of the participants, who are as likely to be chosen by rota, by entitlement or because the course was beneficial to someone else, as by a careful analysis of the learning needs of the potential participant.
4. The lack of time spent adapting the learning acquired on a course to the particular environment in which the teacher operates.

Why use off-the-job training?

Group training, off the job, does, however, have some advantages, especially when used to support, or in conjunction with, 'on-the-job' learning.

- it can provide a sharp, intensive stimulus to learning;
- it can provide knowledge or skill not available on the job;
- it can be designed for intensive, rapid learning;
- it can provide a learning environment outside the daily pressures of school work;
- it can provide the professional spin-off of learning with and from a new group of colleagues;
- it can serve as an alternative to 'on-the-job' learning.

How to get the best from off-the-job training

The influence of the Training Agency, the sharp focus of TVEI and the increasing use of consultants in schools have combined to make courses for teachers more appropriate in design and delivery and increasingly relevant to their needs. To continue this trend my advice would be to:

- expect every teacher to be aware of his or her most effective learning styles;
- use the appraisal system to agree every teacher's chief current learning needs;
- discuss with course organizers what is planned to happen on a proposed course. Consider the extent to which the content matches the needs and styles of the teacher before sponsoring course membership;
- in the design and presentation of courses use only those trainers who are willing to contribute beforehand to analysis and discussion with possible attenders;
- insist on written feedback being given to the trainer and course sponsor from all participants. Require a review session to be built into the course for this purpose;
- build 'on-the-job' experience into the learning of course participants, preferably both before the course and afterwards. Make these planned experiences part of the course, not just reporting-back sessions or mere addenda.

19
LEARNING STYLES

The features of the major learning styles

The importance of the preferred style of learning of the trainee has in recent years, received greater attention in all management training. The concept has tremendous importance for teachers both in their teaching and in their learning. This book concentrates on the latter. It is clear that people learn best in different ways. Most analyses identify four major learning styles, which are variously titled:

1. Converger/activist/enthusiast.
2. Diverger/reflector/imaginative.
3. Assimilator/theorist/logical.
4. Accommodator/pragmatist/practical.

Typical feature of these styles are:

- The activist will experiment with new techniques, uses all the senses, likes to talk things over but dislikes research and logical thought.
- The reflector uses intuition, sees the whole picture and all the alternatives and prefers working out alternatives to deciding on action plans.
- The theorist likes detail, planning and reason but dislikes intuition and risk and is wary of working with others.
- The pragmatist makes plans, wants results, works well alone and likes to solve problems in his or her own way without giving much attention to other ideas.

Matching the style and the learning

Clearly, these styles of operating have implications for the ways in which people learn and how training opportunities should be provided for them. A classification of human relations training and techniques, designed to show the extent of learner involvement, might read as follows:

Reading and private study
Directed reading and study
Lecture and presentation
Interactive presentation
Discussion
Case study
Role play and simulation
Structured experiences
Self-assessment questionnaires
Group counselling.

The activist avoids lectures, theory and too much detail. He or she likes interactive and experiential courses, role playing, structured experiences, management games, competitive team situations, high-profile activities and new challenges.

The reflector avoids unstructured situations, impromptu discussion and role play. He or she likes opportunities to observe, review or research without time pressure or the pressure to perform.

The theorist avoids unstructured situations which lack concept, depth or validation. He or she likes complex theory with time to reason and discuss after reflection.

The pragmatist avoids training for training's sake or where the purpose is not clear. He or she likes special projects and assignments, and practical, experiential courses led by someone with respected experience in fields which really matter.

Those who manage the training of others need to consider the preferred styles of the people they manage before directing, encouraging or supporting them on learning activities. It is equally important that each of us knows our own preferred styles.

20
SIMULATION IN TRAINING AND DEVELOPMENT

Useful forms of simulation

Simulation may be seen as the attempt to re-create certain environmental, interpersonal or other real-life conditions for training and development. Within the ethos of the simulation, participants attempt to face certain conditions, to achieve objectives or to solve problems. Useful forms of simulation are:

1. The dummy run.
This is useful to familiarize people with strategies or routines or to identify running faults before those routines move from theory into full-scale practice.
2. The pilot project.
This is useful to test a hypothesis before moving into practical operation with it.
3. Models and games.
Models and games are a form of simulation which provides a contextual framework into which selected subject matter can be fed. Known variables from the real-life situation are identified and a hypothetical model is set up in which these variables are expected to operate.
4. Structured techniques.
In structured simulation the designers have determined the objectives and the critical relationship with which the participants are to cope. Examples

of these techniques include the 'in-basket' exercise, the partly prepared script which the participants simulate to its conclusion and the assignments with a prepared brief for two or more of the participants.

5. Unstructured simulation techniques.

In unstructured simulation, the objectives and the critical relationship are determined by the participants at the time of the simulation. It is a technique which runs the same risk as all forms of spontaneity, but it gains from tackling real-life problems based on situations that are real to the participants. Examples of such techniques are role reversal (a teacher plays the role of the person he or she found a problem to handle), the Tommy Cooper tactic (the teacher plays both roles, so trying to reconstruct the attitude and actions of both parties) and the 'Now let's try that again with one change' technique, which reconstructs a real-life incident, but with control over one particular, identified condition.

I have used some of these unstructured techniques not only in the formal training situation, but also in 'on-the-job' coaching. For example, with a head of department who could not give due praise for a very good performance to a teacher he actively disliked, we worked together on the 'empty chair' technique, where he rehearsed giving appropriate praise to the teacher. The simulation took place in the departmental head's own room, using the chairs, desk and whole environment in which the interview should have taken place. The only difference was the empty chair. It took him several halting, grudging attempts to give the praise, but eventually he could do so. When the real-life interview took place, the teacher was stunned to receive credit and even celebration where none had been forthcoming before. Within weeks a positive appraising relationship had developed and mutual respect replaced rivalry and mistrust.

Applications of simulation

The applications of simulations are many and varied, but may be broadly classified as follows:

1. Training:
- in specific methods (method-centred training);
- in the skills and principles of human relations (problem-centred training);
- in self-awareness (individual-centred training).
2. Informing (of a principle, a method, a set of facts):
- to demonstrate;

- to emphasize;
- to clarify;
- to deepen understanding.

3. Analysis of:
- how a teacher performs in certain situations;
- how a teacher is likely to perform in certain situations.

Such applications of simulations are as useful in on-the-job coaching as in the formal training situation.

21
USING CONSULTANTS

When to use a consultant

To be a successful leader in a school you do not need to know all there is to know about education and its management. Many headteachers operate successfully knowing little about marketing, the curriculum or financial accounting. The secret is knowing when and where to seek help and how to use it. Use a specialist consultant as a resource for diagnosis or to fill an identified need. Use a consultant:

1. Where the consultant, as part of a planned management of change programme, can raise the awareness of staff for a proposed change, e.g.
   ● make staff aware of the objectives, mechanics and ethos of a staff appraisal system.
2. Where the specialized expertise which the consultants have is not available internally, e.g.
   ● provide skills training for junior staff in handling the record of achievement interview with pupils;
   ● provide skills training for senior staff in appraisal systems and skills.
3. Where the consultants are installing a packaged efficiency improvement of which the training forms an integral part, e.g.
   ● introduce a package to improve the management skills of staff and provide the necessary skills training;
   ● introduce a model for headteacher appraisal, teach the skills, manage the ethos and the early interviews. Be available to review the process.

4. Where the consultant acts as a catalyst and provides the organization with the skill to carry out its own internal training and consultancy, e.g.
   - train trainers to present their PSE (personal and social education) skills to colleagues and to coach them. Devise and support progressively more difficult training opportunities for the trainers. Be available to support their work and to review it;
   - refresh the skills of senior staff in their skills of appraisal. Devise controlled opportunities for them to present these to other senior managers ready for coaching their own staff as appraisal is developed in each school. Be available to support and review;
   - prepare curriculum co-ordinators in schools to be consultants to their heads of faculty and department in securing the delivery of the National Curriculum. Review with the co-ordinators as a group after an agreed interval and support each one individually as required.
5. Where the governors or professional management of a school seek advice on a problem or confirmation of its conclusions prior to implementation:
   - the headteacher management performance appears to be declining and impeding the development of the school; the problem is making the headteacher aware of the specific shortcomings and providing an improvement programme.

22
ENSURING VALUE FOR MONEY IN TRAINING AND DEVELOPMENT

How effective was the experience?

The greatest problem with assessing whether a planned experience provided value for money is the opportunity cost of not being able to compare life without that experience and life with that experience. Gone are the days when any training was thought to be beneficial, and irrelevant, badly delivered courses were experienced by patient teachers who were never expected to give feedback. There is no doubt that the fact that a teacher's manager is sufficiently interested to develop a planned experience will, in itself, have a beneficial effect. But is a more precise evaluation possible?

The first test is 'Did the planned experience match the need it was planned to meet?', in other words did the experience meet its own objectives? Sources of feedback on this test are:

- the participant;
- the trainer or other manager of the experience;
- the planner of the experience, who might be either or both of the above, or a third party;
- the manager of the department in which the participant is to practise the acquired learning.

The second test is 'How valuable was the experience to the trainee and to the school?' Key sources of feedback on this test are:

- the participant;
- the manager of the department in which the participant is to practise the acquired learning;
- the client, who might be a student, a parent, a colleague, a departmental team, etc.

The chief forms of assessment of training effectiveness which school could readily use are:

- cost-benefit analysis
- participant feedback
- post-experience practice
- observation of a third party.

Cost-benefit analysis

Clearly the school would like some simple form of cost-benefit analysis to help it assess the value of planned developmental experiences. Whatever system is used, it must

- be consistent, to allow comparison;
- allow for qualitative judgements, since not all training effectiveness can be quantified;
- consider the opportunity cost of not now being able to spend the funds involved on a different experience;
- consider the cost of staff absence from the teaching room if the experience is run in school time.

Costs will almost inevitably be notional costs – the cost of not inducting new teachers into the ethos and practices of the school is error, inaction and inappropriate style. The cost of not training staff to manage interviews may be aggrieved parents, badly appraised staff and student antipathy to the record of achievement system. To some of these an estimated quantitative cost can be given, for example the cost of the pupil who is withdrawn from the school because of being inappropriately handled. To others – the teacher demotivated after an unsuccessful appraisal interview – the school can only estimate a qualitative cost.

Participant feedback

By far the most common form of training evaluation is by participant feedback. With on-the-job learning teaching, learning and feedback are closely intertwined. If, as a head, I am coaching my deputy in adopting a more appropriate management style in a particular situation, then the activities of explanation, demonstration, practice, discussion and practical feedback follow in appropriate order during the period of the whole planned experience. If an aspect of the experience had been misunderstood, support is readily at hand. If the newly acquired style began to deteriorate in practice, a refresher could be easily organized. With the kind of appraising relationship which is described in Chapter 9, there would also be very little problem with a joint validation of the design of the experience or with appraising its effectiveness. Such feedback is all part of the appraising relationship. But schools should never take feedback for granted. Seek and give feedback as part of a good professional relationship. If it all seems a little too cosy, invite a third party to observe the whole exercise and appraise it. Use a colleague for ease of access; bring in a local inspector or a specialist consultant if the model is important to the school.

Off-site courses do not have the same flexibility for testing in practice, correction or support. Participant feedback from them, therefore, runs the danger of being a 'one-off' appraisal, taken usually at the end of the event. However, feedback can be usefully extended in a number of ways.

1. Session evaluation sheets

Use

These are completed at the end of each session, topic or lecture, usually within minutes of its ending. Frequently the feedback is kept to a minimum and concerns the immediate impact of the session. Along with space for written, free-ranging comment, 'To what extent do you feel that this unit met its objectives?' is a typical question, with a choice of subjective grades:

- completely
- to a large extent
- to some extent
- only slightly
- not at all.

Advantage

It gives opportunity for immediate reaction uncoloured by discussion with other participants. It also prevents one poor item being forgotten in an otherwise good course.

Disadvantage

It is not suitable for aspects of feedback which required greater reflection. Also, the feedback may be influenced by the euphoria factor or by the boredom factor following a particular style of presentation, before there has been opportunity for its content and use to be evaluated.

2. Course evaluation sheets

Use

These are completed at the end of the course, before or after a discussion of course validation and assessment, which should be built into every such event. This evaluation sheet can be given to participants with the pre-course briefing, giving greater opportunity for reflection on a range of validation and assessment issues. The continuum design seeks reaction to specified features, while there is further space for unrestricted comment.

COURSE EVALUATION SHEET

TITLE OF COURSE ....

NAME OF PARTICIPANT ....

DATE ....

For each of the questions 1–5, will you please place a tick above the point on the scale corresponding to the course you have attended.

1. How much did you enjoy the session as a whole?
   Very stimulating ————————————————— Very boring.

2. To what extent have you been able to understand the material presented?
   Completely ——————————————— I found it all rather confusing.

3. How important do you think it is for you to remember what you have learned on this course?
   Extremely important ————————————— Totally unnecessary.

4. To what extent will you be able to apply what you have learned in this session to your job?
   Able to apply most ————————————— Unable to apply any.

5. Please comment on the overall presentation of the session.
   Excellent ————————————————————— Poor.

Please write any other comments below and overleaf if required, e.g. did the session live up to your expectations?

3. Participant total course evaluation

This type of evaluation is more suitable for longer courses and for collecting information on all aspects of the course. It should be completed within about one week of the completion of the course.

Course design

a. Was the course sufficiently well publicized?
b. Was its purpose explained clearly before you joined the course?
c. Was a clear understanding of the aims, content and working style of the course given as a basis for deciding whether or not to attend?
d. Was the pre-reading helpful?
e. How successful was the activity balance of the course? (lecture/practical/discussion/special study)
f. Was the balance of group work about right in individual, pair, triads, small-group and whole-group working?
g. Were the planned breaks about the right length, allowing a prompt start to the next session?
h. What was missing from the course design which you would have liked to have seen there?

Course content

a. How relevant was the subject of the course to you in in your present or proposed future work?
b. What part of the content of the course, if any, could have been omitted?
c. What could have been added to the course content to improve the course?
d. Can you pick out any particularly strong or weak sessions in the course?
e. Were there any parts of the content of the course which you would like to have studied in more detail?

Course style

a. How appropriate was the course style to you as a senior manager in a school?
b. How appropriate did you find the the language of the course?

Course organization and facilities

a. How conducive were the lecture base and activity rooms (e.g. team discussion spaces, video rooms, etc.) to working on the course?
b. How suitable was the general accommodation for a residential course?
c. How effective were the audio-visual aids used on the course?
d. Could other audio-visual aids have been constructively used?
e. How useful were the handouts distributed on the course?
f. How do you rate the social facilities for course members (meals, bar, recreational and rest facilities, etc.)?

Course leadership

a. What effect has the style of leadership of the course leader had on the course?

b. Would a different leadership style have been more appropriate?
c. Did the leader appear to be sufficiently expert in the topic to lead the course?

Members

a. Did you feel the number of course members was too large, too little or about right?
b. Did you feel that members expectations of the course were fairly uniform?
c. Was there sufficient time for members to interact in course activities?
d. Did members have enough opportunity to contribute to the course?

Course achievements

a. Are there tasks which you have to undertake at school which are likely to be tackled more effectively over the next 12 months because of your membership of the course?
b. Has your attitude to people or to any part of your management task been changed by your membership of this course?
c. Is it possible to list any of your chief learning needs which have been met by this course?
d. The aims of this course were as printed on the course brochure. Have these aims been achieved?
e. What would you like to see as a the training follow-up to the work of this course?

4. Course tutors' review

At the end of the course the tutors meet to discuss their impressions of the course in areas similar to those evaluated by participants in their total course review.

5. Course evaluator's report

Within about one month of the ending of a course the course evaluator, using evidence from all of the above sources, including his or her own visits to the course, writes a report. The evaluator may be a tutor on the course or the function may be shared with, or delegated to, an external evaluator.

6. Action programme

Should the course be so designed, members may wish to submit a plan of action and request follow-up support. Such proposals would be co-ordinated by the course tutor, whose responsibility it is to assess feasibility and agree follow-up action with each member requesting it.

7. Long-term evaluation

Twelve months after the ending of the course a further appraisal is taken from course members, with emphasis on the long-term effects of the course. Where an action programme has been undertaken it, too, may be evaluated at this stage. The key questions to be answered are the first three questions in the 'Course achievements' section of the participant total course evaluation (see page 147).

Post-experience practice

The ultimate criterion for the assessment of training is performance on the job. Real-life performance galvanizes in a way that questionnaires cannot. Ideally the focus of the training would be put to the test in the form of a discreet project which required its ample use. So much the better if this can be done. Next best is that the newly honed technique is tested in an easily observable situation such as, for example, the management of meetings. Sometimes, however, the new technique is a style of operating or an inter-personal skill; it may be inappropriate to observe this in action and so assessment may be based on end-results rather than on observing the process. There is much to be said for the Industrial Society's recommendation of the 'action plan', made during the training, when thought is given to how and where the training will meet the learning needs of the teacher. This approach not only makes implementation easier, but also facilitates the review process.

Although all of these post-experience practices are useful, the natural and most effective method in the appraising school is the appraising relationship and performance review. As we saw in our analysis of the methods of highlighting learning needs, individual performance appraisal features as a very important method. It is equally important in assessing the effectiveness of the new technique in operation, both on a day-to-day basis and in summarizing its developing use over time. A deficiency in performance will be discussed at the appraisal interview and will most likely be turned into a target with its own built-in performance criteria. It is these criteria which will help to decide whether the training has filled the performance gap. The use of performance appraisal and of target-setting are discussed in detail later (see Chapter 35).

Observation of a third party

In any of the training evaluation situations described it is possible to introduce a third party to observe and give feedback. Only in an unusual situation is there a need to involve a colleague and inspector or a consultant in this role. Such unusual situations include:

- Where both teacher and appraiser are relatively inexperienced to the new technique, for example in record of achievement interviewing when the teacher has been newly trained in the skill but the appraiser, the head of year, also has limited relevant expertise.
- Where there is conflict or lack of trust between teacher and appraiser and there is fear of an unjust assessment of competence in the new technique.
- Where the school is anxious to show the third party that the new technique is being used effectively. In this case the third party may be a body such as the LEA or the governing body represented by a local inspector or a consultant.

Training records

Whoever is responsible for development and training in the school will need to keep an updated training plan. Over time this will become a training record. The plan must show:

1. How the need was identified, e.g. self, appraisal interview, in line with school training policy, etc.
2. The department for which the training or development is being undertaken, e.g. mathematics, pastoral care, senior managers, etc.
3. Who the trainees are.
4. What the development or training targets are, e.g. basic induction programme, an appreciation of the importance of management styles, the management of meetings, etc.
5. An outline of the experience which is planned, e.g. after hours, in-house course led by a deputy head, delegation within the English department, two-day course led by consultant, etc.
6. Who has responsibility for ensuring the training is appropriately carried out, e.g. self-managed, deputy head (training and development), head of technology department, etc.
7. Period of the training or development, i.e. dates when the planned experience begins and ends, including confirmation of completion.
8. Cost of the planned experience, showing separately the cost of supply cover and the actual training or development costs.

If staff development and training are to be successful in schools, the following are probably the chief factors in their success:

- the commitment, support and involvement of top management, even if that involvement is limited to allowing their own development to be high profile;
- effective and widely understood means of identifying training needs, and of prioritizing them;
- high-quality training throughout the programme, including the ethos, attitude and staff training skills within staff teams for on-the-job learning as well as effective, stimulating trainers and consultants in off-site training;
- the training and development are cost effective rather than cheap;
- evaluation methods which enable development and training to be assessed, adapted and improved.

The aim of performance appraisal is to improve performance. One of the ways it can achieve its purpose is to identify learning needs, define and describe training needs and ensure that they are met. Be certain that people know this is its purpose in the school. Establish the appraiser's role as a coach. Create the essential participative environment. Establish a learning contract through the target-setting process which clarifies the role in teacher development, not only of the teacher, but of the appraiser as well.

23
A NEW ROLE IN TRAINING FOR THE EDUCATION SERVICE

A new role in training and management for LEAs

The residual role described for LEAs in the recent report by the School Management Task Force (DES, 1990) is a much reduced if important one. The role is now sufficiently discreet to be handled by any agency which could deliver the service which schools require. If LEAs are not to hand over this support role to a rival body but are to continue to function, it would appear that they must make some urgent adjustments. Chiefly these adjustments are:

1. Effect an attitude change in which the LEA sees itself as serving the school. Bring about the change as a matter of urgency by exposition, example and redundancy. If LEAs wish to survive they must seek out customer needs and find the means to offer a range of solutions to them.
2. Ensure a change in nature and an improvement in the quality of the skills of the advisory service. This can be achieved both by development and by recruitment, especially in people management and consultancy skills.
3. Replace the traditional, gratuitous, institutionalized and largely outmoded advisory function of the LEA with a range of optional services that are available for schools to purchase.
4. Become an agency to which schools will wish to turn for those external services which the schools need but which the LEA cannot provide. Know what is available for schools outside the LEA in terms of

skills, service, a consultancy and advice. This will in turn sharpen LEA awareness and improve its service as well as saving each school a time-intensive search.

5. Realize that the sharp end of education is the teacher in the classroom. All those who earn a living in education in any other way – LEA administrators, inspectors and officers as well as senior staff in schools – do so in order to support and develop the education of the students. For some this will be a humbling but constructive experience

6. Streamline the communication between school and LEA. Minimize the information sought from schools and speeding the supply of such information to schools as is needed by them to maximize the efficacy of their service.

7. Update the techniques used to collate data on schools, so that school development planning is helped and not hindered by the quality of the competence and effective support of the LEA.

8. Do all that is possible to make the task of school management easier through improved systems and working, even if it makes the task of the LEA more difficult. For many heads in the past the experience has been the opposite: their biggest school problem has been working to make the administrative task of the LEA easier at the expense of effective school management.

9. Provide, as a fixed programme, a small range of essential developmental courses for those wishing to lead schools or lead teams within them. These generic off-site courses are an essential support to the ongoing management development of staff, which is the obligation of the school. A typical range of courses which could be advertised for sale to schools on a consortia or an individual basis might be:
   a. Basic management training, covering the functions of management and appropriate leadership styles. Essential to all who are leading others for the first time.
   b. Management of managers' training, emphasizing the difference between first- and second-line management. Essential to all who are managing other managers for the first time, such as prospective deputy headteachers.
   c. Senior management training, concentrating on the broad perspective necessary for headship and on the essentials of making an organization work.
   d. Specific skill courses which are basic to the teaching profession such as a range of interview, negotiating and interpersonal skills.

10. Provide a flexible service adapted to meet the needs of individual schools, such as:

    a. Programmes of training and consultancy support developed in conjunction with a school to meet its development needs.

    b. Similar programmes to the above, but developed to meet the needs of consortia.

    c. Consultancy, especially in curriculum delivery skills and in people management.

    d. Consultancy available to schools and to teams within them which helps to review their planning of working practices.

    e. Distance learning material to support on-the-job learning.

11. Use the general inspector (GI) role to stay in close personal touch with school achievements, needs, development and strategies. The role of the GI is discussed in detail elsewhere in this book (see page 165).

12. Monitor the LEA services to schools, seek feedback on its quality and efficacy and act on the feedback in order to edit and develop LEA service.

13. Show commitment to these changes from the top of the LEA hierarchy. Begin with a title change to 'head of school support service' instead of existing titles, such as 'director of education', so as to give a more accurate description of function.

It is a longstanding criticism of LEAs that they have allowed the administration of education to dominate the service – the tail is wagging the dog, so to speak. Anthony and Hertzlinger (1980) sum it up as 'A Civil Service syndrome develops as a result of the trait caveat signalled by the system structure. "You need not produce success: you need merely to avoid making major mistakes" '. Given this as a culture, the LEA, the only organization in a position to encourage excellent schools, had no incentive to do so and indeed did not do so. Schools producing a common standard of education, even if it is not a good one, are easier to administer than schools generating the conflict and change that is brought about by striving for excellence. An outstandingly poor school is something of a problem to an LEA, but at least it serves to make the rest appear good. An outstandingly good school, on the other hand, is a thorough pain, casting doubts on the efficacy of all other schools and even on the system itself.

However, this would not be the case if the climate within the LEA were one of service to its schools – if it treated the school as a customer and not as a supplier. For the LEA which wants to meet the developmental needs of its customers, a touch of excellence in any school is something to be welcomed, analysed and replicated. That excellence becomes the focus of staff development for all schools and the conditions in which excellence thrive become a target for the LEA to reproduce in every school.

The parable of the sower

There is the story of the head who so believed that schools could be improved that as soon as his own was agreed to be sound and successful, he tried to stimulate debate about school quality with the senior staffs of other local schools. For two years he ran monthly seminars at his school in the evenings, arranged for each member to make a presentation on an issue of school performance followed by general debate, and sent a printed summary of the distilled professional wisdom of the group to the LEA. In the third year the LEA killed off the debate by sending an adviser to manage the group. It withered in a matter of months.

The head then pioneered management training courses at the local university. These courses were for colleague heads in the region, led by leaders of excellent organizations, and provided training in key skills for the improvement of schools – style flexibility, staff development and interpersonal skills. All this constituted an attempt to show the LEA how it could serve schools and help them to become excellent. The head presented a paper to the LEA on the repertoire it could offer, how it could develop the management of schools and improve the management conditions it created in which schools had to operate. But a body which is preoccupied with staying within its own rules to preserve its own safety and expertise will not seriously consider taking the risk of a new and much humbler role, even if that new role will better serve those who educate.

The head then tried ways of demonstrating that there were approaches in his school which produced positive features – staff appraisal, setting high but achievable targets with all staff, creating the conditions in which teachers can teach, producing a school which pleased parents but not advisers, using Hersey and Blanchard as a shared management language for all, striving for computerized school administration as a service to facilitate not frustrate, promoting development on the job. Limited by its own self-vision the LEA considered that such self-promotion by a school was unprofessional vanity which ran the risk of upsetting other schools. Unable to see a new vision for itself and lacking the skills to participate and the will to listen, the LEA grew increasingly alienated from the head. The head became frustrated by the failure of his vision of best practice becoming common practice, with an enlightened LEA supporting mutual school development. He left the profession. I believe that many other heads could tell a similar story.

The lessons in this tale are legion, but for the LEA a few cautionary notes are sounded. First, LEAs must not expect the seeds of change to be handed to them in a packet complete with planting instructions. They must observe and listen to the people and organizations they serve. If they are to survive they must learn from the above example that the messages sometimes come in the requests and proposals that schools make to their LEA and, sometimes in the obviously positive action being taken by schools independently of the LEA. However, sometimes these messages come in what appears to the LEA to be the negative, destructive activity which a school undertakes. The LEA must develop in its representatives who have contact with schools, not only in the essential school relationship of the GI, all those skills of feedback and disclosure which will be described later in this book (see Chapters 31 and 32). Its only reason for existence is to help schools to analyse their needs and to meet them. If it cannot do this the LEA will go to the wall.

24
HEADTEACHER APPRAISAL

A weakness in the Education Reform Act

The Education Reform Act 1988 has initiated one of the greatest revolutions ever experienced by British education. It has tackled all the key problems that face organizations which do not have profit as a motive: identifying the task, measuring output, management skill development, absence of market forces and resource allocation. The whole package of reforms provides a framework for improvement:

- local management of schools (LMS)
- National Curriculum and assessment
- open enrolment
- management by governors
- teacher appraisal and development.

The Education Reform Act has tackled all the key problems except one. On the issue of the management and appraisal of the performance of headteachers it has produced a model with a fundamental weakness. It has continued to leave no one responsible for the day-to-day management of the headteacher's performance; the headteacher has no one with whom to form the appraising relationship. No one can be identified as the manager of the headteacher – not the governors, the LEA nor any member of the inspectorate. I have rehearsed this argument too many times to repeat it here (Trethowan, 1981, 1986, 1989a). The problem now is to live with the structure and to find the management model which does the most to optimize and support headteacher performance.

A model for headteacher appraisal

The model accepts that for a number of reasons it will be difficult to find an appropriately experienced appraiser for headteachers. In all six LEAs involved in the Schoolteacher Appraisal Pilot Study, the person most frequently used as appraiser for teachers was their line manager – either the headteacher, a member of the senior management team or a head of department. However, no similar model could be devised for headteacher appraisal. The peculiar structure of the education service in England and Wales means that unlike every other member of the school staff, the head has no line management superior. The LEAs involved describe their struggle with this concept and their resulting models may be summarized thus:

Cumbria

The school's inspector/adviser worked in collaboration with a practising head from a panel of heads.

Newcastle

Some recommended that a headteacher's appraiser should have relevant experience to headship. This would allow another person with relevant managerial experience to be the main appraiser.

Salford

Four models of headteacher appraisal were piloted:

1. validated peer appraisal;
2. two appraisers (project member plus head);
3. two appraisers (project member plus adviser);
4. one appraiser.

Somerset

Both reviewers allocated to the head are practising headteachers. They involve the appropriate officer/adviser giving contextual information about the school.

Suffolk

Appraisal carried out by a headteacher, the AEO (Area Education Officer) and the school's link adviser. As lead appraiser the consultant head carried the main burden of responsibility for collecting and collating data and for carrying out the dialogue.

The most consistent feature of these pilot headteacher appraisals is the use of a practising colleague head to assume the role of appraiser. Some difficulties with this concept are:

- the lack of responsibility of the appraiser for the headteacher's performance;
- the lack of day-to-day contact to build an appraising relationship;
- the lack of continuously accumulated knowledge of the daily performance of the head;
- the inappropriateness of one head observing sufficient of the performance of another to build an accurate view of performance;
- the issue of appraiser choice, e.g.
  - a friend who might conduct an easy appraisal,
  - a rival who might have scant interest in improving the performance of the head;
- the difficulty of collecting data on headteacher performance in the school of another head;
- the difficulty for the senior management team of a school to give feedback on performance of their leader to another head;
- the lack of priority of time for one head to appraise continuously the performance of another.

Clearly, there is a strong case for all headteachers to 'be answerable to a clearly indicated manager using undisputed criteria for assessment and accepted performance standards supported by annual reviews' (Trethowan, 1981). I have advocated many times the use of the post of school superintendent, whose 'key role would be to appraise the headteacher's performance' (Trethowan, 1981). The superintendent would be responsible for that performance in just the same way as any other appraiser in the system is responsible for the performance of those whom he or she appraises. Governors could expect the superintendent to assist with the process of setting, monitoring and reviewing school targets and to build an appraising relationship with the head as a basis for headteacher performance appraisal. As the School Management Task Force says: 'In a period of increasing autonomy for schools, we do not see a strengthening of LEA line management as the best way to improve headteacher development'.

Clearly the climate is not appropriate for the model used in almost all other advanced nations; its time will come if autonomy fails to deliver and when society is so convinced of the importance of a national education system that it sees national and central accountability and control as a small price to pay for such important ends. In the meantime the task is to maximize the effectiveness of a system which has a nationally imposed curriculum, teachers employed by the local authority and the autonomous school managed by lay governors. It is little wonder that we have a problem with head teacher appraisal!

A practical scheme which can be recommended is one in which

- the principle of a 'colleague head' is retained, but in the role of chairperson, counsellor and clarifier rather than researcher and appraiser;
- the local education authority is represented by a general inspector who has an increasingly important and widely used role in managing the LEA's input into a specific school;
- the head receives feedback from senior staff and from the LEA to add to self-appraisal, before the triad review of performance and the agreement of targets.

The relationship usually begins with an appraisal meeting and develops through the year as targets progress or fail to do so. A strong bond of mutual trust and support has been built up where this scheme has been implemented, much more in the nature of the all-important appraising relationship than of an annual assessment. The keys to the successful development of this relationship are:

1. The retraining of all those involved in the interview in appraisal interview skills and the development of new skills which are appropriate to the handling of a 2:1 appraisal, rather than the more usual 1:1. Opportunity to practise the review skills in simulation is also recommended.
2. The requirement to provide feed back on the positives of the performance as well as on the negatives.
3. The pairing of headteachers (preferably those not in close and direct competition with each other) to encourage mutual disclosure.
4. The clarification of the GI role in relation to the school as a whole and not only for the purposes of appraisal.
5. The importance of the confidentiality of the discussion, even if the agreed targets are relayed to the governing body.
6. The significance of realistic target-setting and of employing the appropriate criteria to establish when a target has been achieved.
7. Recognition of the importance of taking time away from the job to reflect on performance, receive and collate feedback and plan action in the form of targets. Time spent reflecting on the effects of the head's own performance is an essential of the job.

8. Appraised heads can feel a sense of ownership of the scheme, for neither of the other two parties is in a position to force targets on the appraised head.
9. The 'no surprises' rule, which applies to all appraisals, makes it necessary to hold pre-appraisal meetings, often with only two of the three people. The proviso at these meetings is that the appraised head is never discussed in his or her absence by the other two – the 'talk to me, not about me' rule.
10. A previously agreed agenda will be found useful by some heads, although others may find it threatening or restricting.

Roles in the headteacher appraisal interview

Each of the three people involved in the interview process has a defined role. Experience has shown that the most effective distribution of talk is about 60:20:20, where the 60 per cent is the talking contribution of the head being appraised.

Brief for the colleague head

1. The purpose of the appraisal is to help the head to maintain or improve his or her performance.
2. Your role is to manage the meeting and maintain a positive, participative atmosphere. Set up the room. Open and close the meeting.
3. Ensure that both the GI and the head give and listen to feedback fully and sensitively. Help them to say what they want to say. Feed in any information you have which is relevant.
4. Balance criticism and praise:
   - Criticism: concentrate on weaknesses which can be acted on. However, help the head to accept justified criticism.
   - Praise: give genuine praise for achievement. Beware of skipping over this positive part of the session.
5. Do not allow the session to become a power struggle, an academic debate, a point-making contest (like a media interview of a government minister) or a defence of poor practice.
6. Agree which are the two or three high performance areas in the work of the head and the two or three areas where greatest improvement could be made.
7. Be sure the head has ample opportunity to propose his or her own solutions to any problem areas. They will be much easier to accept than any which another person attempts to force on the head.

8. Encourage the head to form any proposed solutions into targets. See that these are clearly presented and meet the target-setting criteria.
9. Complete the target documentation together. Give it to the head to reflect on before he or she finally agrees to take it up as a target.
10. Thank the GI and the head and close the meeting.

Brief for the general inspector

The role of the general inspector at the appraisal of the head must be similarly clarified.

1. The purpose of the appraisal is to help the head maintain or improve his or her performance.
2. Your particular role is to present feedback on the head's performance, together with evidence to support the feedback. Present it in a form which he or she can handle. Concentrate on matters which can be changed.
3. You are trying to agree two or three high performance areas in the work of the head, and two or three areas where performance could be improved.
4. Listen sensitively to what is being said. Although this session is primarily for the head, you may glean information on your own performance or that of the LEA which could help to improve the education service.
5. The head will try to identify solutions and to turn these into targets. You can help with suggestions, with a supportive attitude and with resources if these are appropriate.

Brief for the head

The role of the head being appraised must also be clarified.

1. The purpose of the appraisal is to help you to maintain or improve your performance.
2. Collect together all your ideas and feelings about how effectively you perform your job. Back these up with instances or evidence wherever possible.
3. To help you build up a rounded view of your performance you have the help of:
   - a colleague head who will manage the meeting;
   - your school GI who has collated his or her own feedback and that of the LEA;
   - feedback on your performance from your own senior staff. This has been collated by the consultant and is known only to you.

4. In the meeting listen sensitively to the feedback from others. Ask for clarification of the feedback if you are unsure of any point. Understand it before you react to it.
5. In the meeting, identify two or three areas of your own performance of which you are proud and two or three problem areas where your performance could improve. Consider possible solutions to the problems and turn the solutions you select into targets.
6. The colleague head will work with you, if you wish, to draft out the targets you wish to tackle in the year ahead, making sure they meet the target-setting criteria. Consider your total workload. Take on enough work to continue your development, but not so much that you become overloaded with targets.

In this particular scheme it is helpful to group the heads into pairs. This encourages the appraising relationship and particularly fosters an atmosphere in which a head is more likely to disclose and discuss professional problems. Mutual respect for confidentiality is more likely where each holds some confidences of the other. The GI, as the representative of the LEA which is bound to monitor the appraisal process, can serve as a brake on the appraisal becoming cosily ineffective.

The effectiveness of systems is not shown at their extremes. At one extreme, an effective, aware, improving headteacher will use this 'appraisal' system to develop and improve personal performance. At the other extreme, the head who consistently and blatantly refuses to improve in identified 'areas of focus' will eventually reach the position of a discipline interview with the governing body – (a position he or she should have reached in any case, without the aid of appraisal legislation) – and face dismissal. What the British system of education management denies to the headteacher whose performance lies between those extremes is someone with whom to develop a true appraising relationship with all which that implies for day to day development, support, target programming and for continuous responsibility for the headteacher's performance. My proposal for this role is a School Superintendent with line management relationship with the headteacher. What we have been provided with under the 1991 regulations is a pair of non-line professionals to hold up a mirror to the Headteacher to stimulate and enhance self appraisal. It will take great patience and consummate interactive skills to make it effective. Yet, if headteacher appraisal does not work, the whole teacher appraisal system will lose credibility not only with teachers but with the public, our customers, as well.

25
SOURCES OF FEEDBACK FOR HEADTEACHER APPRAISAL

Feedback from senior staff

Headteacher appraisal is appraisal of the performance of the headteacher. It is not to be confused with the performance of the school, which is examined in a school review. Each may refer to the other in the course of discussion, since they are inevitably bound up, but the targets which emerge from headteacher performance appraisal should be personal targets for the head and not targets for the school.

The key role of the head which must be addressed in an appraisal, is the head's management performance. Heads may take on many other tasks, such as being the publicity agent for the school, being the industrial liaison officer or being a teacher in one of the departments of the school. Important as these functions are, they are optional for the head. The head can choose to delegate them to others or to undertake them. If they are undertaken then an appropriate means of appraisal will need to be devised for them so that the head may be aware of his or her degree of success. But the function of appropriately managing the senior management team is not an optional one. Yet without a manager how can the head obtain feedback on his or her managerial success?

Clearly, the people who know best how the head is performing are those on the receiving end of that performance – the senior colleagues who are directly accountable to, and are managed directly by, the headteacher. In the appraising school, senior colleagues expect to give the head regular feedback on performance, but in many schools it is still difficult for the head to be given balanced feedback from colleagues. In our headteacher appraisal model, a consultant is appointed to collect from senior staff comments on all aspects of the managerial performance of the head. These are given individually and in confidence to the consultant; they are views purely from the personal experience of the colleague. He or she is asked 'How far do you feel your headteacher carries out the specific functions which are to be described, in relation to you?' The consultant undertakes never to disclose this individual feedback to anyone, including the head. The consultant collates the feedback from all senior colleagues and presents the composite view of his or her performance to the head.

This composite document in turn remains confidential to the head unless the head wishes to disclose all or part of it at any time. The most fruitful occasion to disclose it is in the appraisal interview, when it can be used to identify, to reject or to support the targets which are emerging. But the decision on whether to reveal this confidential perception of performance lies with the head. Its value is that it gives an insight into both positive and negative aspects of performance which the head might not otherwise have gained.

The aspects of management on which the heads receive feedback are as follows:

- Planning
- Organization
- Control
- Delegation
- Facilitation of working
- Decision-making
- Communication
- Consideration of the colleague as an individual
- Motivation
- Recognition of contribution
- Development.

The form and range of the feedback which result from this collation and analysis process are unlikely to be presented to the head through any other means than through feedback from senior staff. This feedback is invaluable in compiling a perception of performance, the more so when the lack of a line manager denies the head an input which industrial managers in a similar position regularly receive.

The role of governors in headteacher appraisal

The governing body or its nominated member can assist the appraisal process by:

- agreeing with the head how feedback from the governing body is best included in the appraisal. Most heads prefer a discussion with the chairperson, with the feedback remaining confidential in the same way as that from the senior staff.
- expecting to see the agreed targets of headteachers, as of other staff.
- ensuring that the system of appraisal is operating effectively, for heads as well as for all staff. The efficient operation of the system is the responsibility of the LEA, but the interest of the governors in the effectiveness of the system can have nothing but a positive effect.
- allowing the content of appraisal discussions to remain with those professionals who must necessarily be party to them. It will undoubtedly inhibit the full and proper flow of feedback and disclosure between the participants if governors cannot show this respect.
- expecting the nominated governor to be willing to listen to the grievance of a senior member of staff who is dissatisfied with his or her appraisal. The usual practice in such cases is for a dissatisfied teacher to 'leapfrog' his or her immediate appraiser and seek redress with the appraiser's appraiser. Those teachers appraised directly by the head do not have this privilege except by the active participation of an appropriate governor or the LEA.

The role of the school general inspector

An important factor in increasing the LEA's awareness of school needs as well as in fulfilling its role of school monitoring and support, is the recent increase in the appointment of a general inspector (GI) to each of its schools. GIs normally work with one or two secondary schools, together with a number of primary schools frequently grouped in the secondary school catchment area. It is quite common for these local inspectors to be operating without a job description and to be developing this important role by trial and error. Discussion with people who hold the role and with those in schools most likely to receive the services of a GI, leads to the following role analysis, on which a job description may easily be based.

Role analysis for a general inspector

Support school problem-solving

1. Help the school to find answers to its problems in line with its stated objectives.
2. Stimulate the school to think of alternative solutions to problems.

3. Discuss school problems with the appropriate member of staff.
4. Help the school to work within its management strategy.
5. Help the school to review the success of its solutions to problems.

Support the development of staff

1. Help the staff to develop appropriate skills for their present post.
2. Help with the development of new and probationary staff.
3. Help the school to improve the performance of the poor performer.
4. Offer advice to staff which is appropriate in view of their school performance.
5. Help the staff to prepare for appropriate responsibility in the future.

Support headteacher self-development

1. Encourage the head in difficult tasks.
2. Listen when the head wants to talk through a problem.
3. Help the head with self-appraisal and review of performance.
4. Help the head to set realistic personal targets.
5. Regularly give the head feedback on the head's own performance.

Recognize achievement

1. Be fair in evaluating school achievements.
2. Recognize the contribution of individuals to school achievement.
3. Detect good work.
4. Acknowledge and celebrate good work.
5. Know well all members of the school staff.

Demonstrate reliability

1. Keep any promises made to staff in schools.
2. Fulfil any commitments made to schools.
3. Be willing to back schools up wheu they need support.
4. Reliably pursue answers to queries raised by schools.
5. Maintain a previously defined quality service in returning calls and messages.

Monitoring and evaluation

1. Keep a careful eye on as much as possible of each allocated school.

2. Keep school in touch with any national or LEA requirements.
3. Help schools to analyse and evaluate their examination results.
4. Monitor the progress of schools towards the delivery of the National Curriculum and of their own set targets.
5. Bring an LEA-wide perspective to school monitoring and evaluation.

Organization and time management

1. Organize well his or her own work.
2. Manage meetings well.
3. Make time for discussion with individual staff on personal problems.
4. Attend most school events.
5. Show interest in as many facets as possible of those events attended.

Work facilitation

1. Help schools to use the finance, staff and other resources to do the job.
2. Use experience and knowledge to help the work of the school.
3. Be available when staff need advice or support.
4. Plan appropriate training with and for school staff.
5. Broaden staff perspective by helping them keep in touch with appropriate initiatives.

Planning

1. Help schools to set realistic aims.
2. Help the schools to formulate strategic plans.
3. Help to make successful appointments to schools.
4. Agree the ground rules for the general inspector's role.
5. Be involved in school development planning.

Consideration

1. Listen to staff when they have something to say.
2. Give honest feedback sensitively.
3. Be sensitive to school relationships and issues.
4. Give realistic and sensitive interview debriefing if required to do so by the school.
5. Give any negative feedback to staff in a form which they can accept.

Representation

1. Represent fairly the school to the LEA and vice versa.
2. Represent fairly the school to the governors and vice versa.
3. Represent fairly the position of any individual within the school to any higher authority.

The model described above is permissible under the 1991 School Teacher Appraisal Regulations, but is not the only model which can be devised under them. In providing any model, some key questions on which the LEA or other 'appraising body' under the 1991 regulations must provide guidance are:

- Who manages the appraisal?
- Who carries out its administration?
- How are areas of focus to be identified?
- How is an agenda agreed?
- To whom in practice is the appraisal statement confidential?
- What happens when the target setting is abused with soft, irrelevant targets or with no targets at all?
- What happens when targets have not been achieved?

The means of providing a suitable 'colleague head' include pairing, selection from a cadre of experienced practising heads or the appointment of one or two former heads to the post of 'appraising colleague head'. Avoid any version of a rota. Whatever the system, the key to its success is a continuing relationship. The closer the relationship between the appraisers can approximate to a continuous appraising of trust, understanding and honesty, the more it is likely to succeed and the less likely any of the above questions are to become issues. But that relationship has one overwhelming difference from all other appraisals in schools in that neither of the appraisers of a headteacher is in a management relationship with the head. The adviser represents the body responsible for the appraisal system, not for headteacher performance, whilst the colleague head is little more than an innocent bystander. What they offer is not appraisal, but purely feedback on performance. In true appraisal there is a managerial obligation to ensure that performance is maintained or improved. What the British headteacher experiences under the 1991 regulations is at best the possibility of enhanced self appraisal – assistance with the clearer definition of 'areas of focus', with their translation into targets and with the confirmation of target achievement.

26
HEADTEACHER APPRAISAL INTERVIEWING

Session format for the initial setting of targets

The following format is appropriate for an initial session between two headteachers and a GI, discussing and setting targets.

Head's target-setting session

Climate/opening

The colleague head has the responsibility of setting an appropriate participative, trusting climate giving special attention to assuring the head of support. To obtain the best from the session the head must feel that he or she can disclose concerns in confidence and be supported in developing solutions for improvement.

The colleague head also sets the scene and reiterates the purpose of the meeting and of the ensuing exercise. Encourage the head to identify his or her own strengths. It can be as important that the head knows which strong areas of his or her own performance have to be maintained as it is to search for areas in which to improve. Also, discussion of these positive areas produces a better balance in the session. Follow this with a structured exploration.

Exploration

1. The head's self-selected positive and negative points. About three of each will be sufficient. This form of appraisal does not lend itself easily

to a full review of performance, but concentrates on maintaining the best and improving the worst.

2. The general inspector's positive and negative points. About three of each will be sufficient. Some of these are likely to be the same as those selected by the head. If so, this strengthens the appraisal when the views of the head are supported or added to by another professional. But the meeting may also review the reasons for the comparative priority of the points.

3. Any appropriate analysis of these points. The analysis may take the form of clarification of the points raised, or may develop into a review of causes and effects.

4. The head's personal needs and aspirations. Even headteachers may have career development needs, such as the need to develop certain skills little used in headship as well as personal needs for performance improvement.

5. Future job requirements. Is it possible to foresee a change in the head-teacher's role for which the head could now be preparing? If so, this may form the basis of a target.

Agree development areas

Having explored the ground of the headteacher's present performance and likely future role, the next stage is to agree with the head which of these areas will be selected for action.

1. Acknowledge any suggestions the head has to make. As with the exploration of performance, self-suggested development areas tend to sustain greater commitment than those which are seen as being 'forced' on the head. Bear in mind that even if the appraisal process is compulsory, the amount of effort put into the achievement of targets is decided by the target-holder.

2. Allow the general inspector and the colleague head to contribute their views. Build on these and support them where appropriate. Add proposals where the head seems to be overlooking an important area, but beware of having too many proposals in the discussion since this gives the 'walking through treacle' feeling that the meeting is not making progress. Make sure disagreements concern content, not personalities.

3. Discuss the benefits and drawbacks of the proposed development areas. Some will be costly in time and effort for little return. In other cases a small investment in time and energy may vastly improve the effectiveness of the head or of those he or she manages.

4. Finally, agree the areas to be developed. Keep the number of areas small – between two and five is ideal. Remember that each development area might contain several targets.

Set the targets

1. Agree a course of action in each development area.
2. Turn the action plans into targets, each with its own performance criteria which answer the question 'How will I know when I've done it?'
3. Remind the head that the colleague and the general inspector are willing to discuss or support progress at any mutually agreed time.

Close

1. Agree a review date.
2. Redirect the head back to his or her agreed key positive achievements.
3. Thank the participants.

Session format for reviewing targets

The following format is appropriate for a session between two headteachers and a GI, reviewing targets either at an agreed date during the target period or at its end.

Head's review session

Climate/opening

The colleague head has the responsibility of setting an appropriate participative, trusting climate, recalling the purpose of the meeting and the need for understanding and honesty.

The review is best opened by asking the head to comment on his or her own view of the success with the set targets. Once the viewpoint of the head has been listened to and understood, it will not be difficult to stimulate interactive comment.

Review of the targets

1. Check the targets against their definition and performance criteria. The interest of no one is served by being lax in this operation.
2. Use disclosure and feedback to agree
   - that the target has been achieved;
   - that appropriate progress is being made;
   - that there has been little or no progress.

Analysis

1. Explore how and at what cost the targets were achieved.
2. When and why they were shelved?

3. Were the targets overtaken by events?
4. What took their place?
5. Did priorities change?
6. Were the chosen targets never really relevant and important?

Develop the self-improvement plan

1. Reset the targets with new deadlines and criteria.
2. Set new targets, ensuring that they meet the target-setting criteria.

Close

1. Fix a new review date.
2. Thank the participants.

27
SKILLS TRAINING FOR HEADTEACHER APPRAISAL

A basic skills course

Any skills course for the form of headteacher appraisal which is being discussed here should be undertaken by not more than three of the triads which have been formed to conduct the appraisals. About 10 people is sufficient for an intensive skills course, and since the pair of headteachers may not have the same GI the number of participants can vary from 9 to 12. The skills course is best undertaken a month or two before the appraisal. It can be handled successfully in one and a half days. An outline course for such headteacher appraisal work is given below, together with a suitable role-play exercise.

Basic skills course for headteacher appraisal

Day one

16.30 Introductions. The consultant may not be known to the whole group and possibly they do not all know each other. Restate the purpose of the exercise and the role of the skills course within it.

17.00 Essentials of appraisal. The consultant presents the basic requirements of an appraisal system, pointing out where headteacher appraisal necessarily differs from teacher appraisal.

17.30 Discussing the system. Free-ranging discussion to ensure fears, reservations and misunderstandings are expressed and resolved.

18.30 Summarizing the system. The consultant summarizes the system, including any refinements which have now been agreed by the group.
19.00 Close. Dinner followed by an evening for the triads to build their relationships.

Day two

09.00 Consultant identifies the key appraisal skills, illustrating their use in headteacher appraisal.
10.00 Skills practice exercises.
11.00 Coffee.
11.15 Video of appraisal skills in action.
11.45 Briefing and preparation for role play.
12.15 Lunch.
13.30 Role play.
14.30 Role-play review and its relevance to the forthcoming appraisal (see below).
15.30 Final details of the scheme and its requirements are summarized by the consultant.
16.00 Close.

A role play to develop appraisal skills

The following briefing is for a role play to be used for skills practice by the three participants in headteacher appraisal.

1. Brief for the colleague head: Lance E. Lott

The brief for the colleague head is given in Chapter 26.

2. Brief for the general inspector: Alan Merlin

The feedback you want to offer on the strongest and least strong features of Arthur King's performance as headteacher of Camelot Comprehensive is as follows. It has been collated from a GRIDS-type whole school review, the results of which the headmaster is fully aware. You led the review three months ago. To the lessons gleaned from that review you can add comments from the people indicated and your own observations.

Strongest areas

a. Creating a sound ethos
At a time of fairly low morale with teachers generally, Arthur King has

worked hard to give the school a positive climate. This has been commented on at governors' meetings, presented to you in writing by the chairman of governors, was cited by 11 of the 33 sets of parents who opted for Camelot from outside the catchment area and has been drawn to your attention by the subject advisers for mathematics, science, home economics and physical education. All four thought the positive ethos of the school was due to the way Arthur King managed the staff and was 'around' the school to give positive feedback or support whenever appropriate.

b. Planning and control

From the same sources, except for parents, comes the feedback that the school has never been as well planned. Arthur King has worked with his deputies to produce a structured strategic plan and a communication system which runs from a five-year plan down to weekly team briefings by all department heads for their departmental staffs. He is always pressing the LEA for up-to-date information to feed into the school system. As a consequence, staff at Camelot seem better informed than staff at any other school in the authority.

c. Review and improvement of performance

Over the past two years Arthur King has worked with senior staff to encourage his staff to think about their work and how it could be improved. Heads of department annually review the performance of their teams with them according to a well-designed and well-received staff appraisal system. Heads of department are appraised by the deputy headteachers and Arthur King reviews the performance of each member of the senior management team. You know this from your own observations and from a report received from the LEA appraisal co-ordinator. Arthur King has already been given this feedback.

All the above three areas, in your view, deserve recognition and high praise.

Least strong areas

From your own visits to the school, as well as the other sources already mentioned, you would like Arthur King to consider the following areas as target areas for the coming year. Performance in these areas represents probably the least effective areas of his performance.

a. Appointments procedure

Surprisingly, in such a well-organized school, appointments to the staff follow no proper routine at all. There is always a job description, but seldom a person specification. There is no proper briefing of governors for the interview, and candidates seem to be looked after by any member of staff. The opinion of the LEA subject inspector is frequently ignored and sometimes not even sought. Also, when a vacancy occurs there seems to be little opportunity taken to consider restructuring. Feedback on this has come to you from three subject inspectors (languages, science and art) as well as from the chairman of governors. The latter also made his views known to Arthur King, whereas the three inspectors did not.

b. No movement towards the long-term plan for organizational structure
Although there is a long-term school plan for the structure and organization of staff, little opportunity is being taken to implement the changing responsibilities or to move towards the new structure. This lack of implementation came out strongly in the whole school review which you led three months ago, and it reflects the feeling among some staff and governors.

c. Improving the school environment
Although much effort has gone into improving staff morale and general school ethos, this is not reflected in the physical environment of the school. The school was rather run down before Arthur King came to it three years ago, but while he has improved many aspects of school life, no effort seems to have been put into improving the environment. The chairman of governors has raised this with you, but not too strongly, and he has made his views known to the head. The architect's department tell you that it is one of their worst-maintained schools, a view they have not shared with the head.

3. Brief for the headteacher: Arthur King

Your proposals for your strongest and least strong performance areas as head of Camelot Comprehensive came from your own self-appraisal, your perceptions drawn from the whole school review recently led by Alan Merlin, the general inspector, and feedback from the senior staff team collected, collated and presented to you by a consultant. You are keen to listen to the views of Alan Merlin and to develop realistic targets for improving performance.

Strongest areas

a. Leadership of the senior management team
The consultant's survey of the views of senior staff confirms that, in their opinion, you are very sound in planning, organization, delegation, work facilitation, consideration, motivation and development. This feedback is known only to you.

b. Planning and organization

You feel proudest of the way you have been able to draw together practical plans for the school which give expression to the declared aims of the school. This involves various strategies from a five-year plan to weekly briefings by middle management to their teams.

c. Staff development

You and your deputies have worked to set up a staff development system which incorporates staff appraisal and is linked to the school INSET budget. The system and your own involvement in it have done much to confirm to staff that someone actually cares about them and their development.

Least strong areas

The following areas are the ones into which you would like to put the effort for your personal development and professional improvement in the year ahead.

a. Decision-making

It was rather a surprise to you to know that your senior staff questioned your ability to make good, swift decisions when under pressure. You had always felt that speedy decisions were the hallmark of good leadership and had tried to adhere to this. After discussion with the consultant it became clear that some of your decisions were too speedy and might have been better received if they had been delayed a little and more thought given to their likely consequences. Also, you tend to become impatient when any of the senior staff team appears indecisive. On reflection you believe there may be something in what your senior staff are saying and you would like to improve in this area.

b. Improving the school environment

You are aware that the school environment is not as it should be, but you decided some time ago that there were greater priorities. Now, with many other targets achieved, it may be time to put special efforts into improving the school environs and into educating pupils to preserve them.

c. A third target?

Although you could pick a third area, you believe it will be sufficient to add only two targets to the task of maintaining all you have achieved. You would take on a third target if you were convinced of the need by what happens in the forthcoming appraisal meeting.

PART IV
PERFORMANCE
APPRAISAL

28
RESEARCH PREPARATION FOR APPRAISAL INTERVIEWING

The futility of the one-off appraisal

We have already demonstrated the importance of knowing that appraisal is a relationship; it is a method of managing and of being managed. It is day-to-day support, it is continuous staff development, it is agreeing high but achievable targets and it is the management of the conditions in which teachers work. Appraisal means being in and around the teacher's work to catch the teacher 'doing something right'. It means being available for advice and support when things go wrong. It means understanding the task which the teacher is undertaking – its purposes, its place in the total education of the child and its peculiar local difficulties. It means that someone, in addition to the teacher, is directly, personally and continuously responsible for the teacher's performance.

The development of the appraising relationship in the appraising school has been the message of this book. It is only in the context of such a relationship that appraisal interviewing makes sense. As a one-off inspection and assessment it is false, shallow and probably counter-productive. As a natural summary of all that has been achieved in the teacher's year it is the most powerful motivator ever developed. It tells me, as a teacher, that my performance matters, my contribution matters and that I matter. It allows me to form the organization's view of my work in the year which has passed and it helps me to plan my professional work for the year ahead. The relationship and the review are fundamental to the success of appraisal. We have examined how the appraising school builds its relationships. Now it is time to examine in detail the professional skills of the appraisal interview.

The four key appraisal documents

Four key documents will help to make the appraisal interview a success. They are documents with which both appraiser and teacher are familiar. They are not secret documents and they are available to teacher and appraiser at any time of year, not only at the review time. Nothing can be recorded on them without the knowledge of both appraiser and teacher, and what is written is confidential to an agreed small circle of colleagues. The documents are:

1. Description of the system
2. Performance awareness document
3. Target document
4. Basic task of the teacher.

1. Description of the System

When the appraisal system is first set up, openly and clearly describe what are its purposes, procedures and practices. Written in user-friendly language this description not only informs newcomers of the system but reassures and reminds established users of its strengths and limitations. It makes an abuse of the system easier to correct. It helps to ensure that a system designed to be fair is operated fairly.

The description should cover:

- The purpose of the system:
  - maintenance or improvement of present performance;
  - development for future needs.
- The key procedures:
  - the appraising relationship;
  - the establishing of achievements and under-achievements;
  - the importance of self-appraisal;
  - the participative nature;
  - the role of appraisal in the development of all staff.
- The practices to be followed:
  - the collection of data to inform the discussion;
  - the essential preparation for interview;

- the courtesies of its timing;
- guidance on the interview itself;
- how targets are agreed;
- confidentiality routines;
- what happens if an appraisal breaks down.

Trite as it may sound, schools should be sure to write a document which describes their own system and the way they wish it to function. Beware of borrowing a description; make the description fit the system not the system fit the description.

2. Performance awareness document

This is the document which staff sometimes refer to as the 'warm-up' document for that is indeed its chief purpose – to encourage the teacher to warm to the theme of self-appraisal. It encourages self-appraisal. It focuses on the teacher's perception of performance and of developmental needs, related both to present performance and to foreseeable changes. It also seeks the teacher's opinion on the conditions under which he or she functions, and seeks a personal opinion on the organization itself. It asks the teacher to consider such matters as:

- career plan;
- further education or training undertaken;
- specific highlights of the year which have been particularly rewarding, satisfying and positive;
- specific problems, difficulties or experiences which have been unsatisfactory to the teacher;
- proposals for support, courses, 'in-house' coaching or self-improvement plans for personal or professional development;
- suggestions for improving the school or comments on its positive features which should be retained;
- any other matters the teacher would like to discuss.

At the end of this chapter are included two examples of documents to stimulate self-appraisal (see page 189–90). They are: the document used for 15 years at Warden Park School and the document produced as Annexe B of the ACAS report.

The disposal of the performance awareness document should be entirely left to the discretion of the teacher. It is a contradiction in ethos, if not in terms, to want compulsory self-appraisal. The document which is aimed at stimulating self-appraisal might legitimately find the teacher deciding to:

a. Throw it away without using it at all. This is sometimes done by teachers who are familiar with appraisal and feel they do not need to be reminded to consider all aspects of their work before going into an appraisal interview. However, that teacher does need some form of *aide-mémoire* to ensure that all the issues he or she planned to raise are discussed. Teachers would be unwise not to conduct some form of self-analysis of their performance prior to an appraisal, whether or not they chose to use the school document for the purpose.

b. Complete all or part of the document and retain it as a personal crib sheet during the interview.

c. Complete all or part of the document and give it (or a photocopy) to the appraiser so that he or she has a better perception of the teacher's viewpoint. If given to the appraiser a few days before the interview, it allows an opportunity for consideration and reflection. If given to the appraiser during the interview, it can be a distraction as the appraiser tries to conduct the interview while reading or assimilating the important new data.

d. Give the document to the appraiser beforehand but take it back at the end of the interview, either because of its personal nature or because its contents were overtaken by events at the interview. With some imagined conflict now clarified, the teacher may prefer to take away the document in which it was first raised.

e. Give the document to the appraiser and request that it be retained with all other appraisal documentation. This may be because the teacher wants to be sure that his or her views are recorded in exactly the way he or she chooses.

The appraiser, therefore, may have available the teacher's performance awareness document for either the previous year or for the current year, but might equally well have both or possibly neither. A valuable insight into the teacher's view is lost to the appraiser if he or she has not been able to study it. It is also a means for the teacher not only to put forward items which he or she would like to discuss in the interview, but also to state a viewpoint beforehand in writing.

3. Target document – previous year's targets

Whether you are appraiser or teacher you need to examine your copy of the targets which were agreed for the previous year with the teacher, and consider to what extent you believe that they have been achieved. This will not be the first time that either of you has looked at these targets during the year.

As the appraiser you have checked on progress several times, congratulating or offering support. As the teacher you have been trying to achieve the targets, self-monitoring by keeping an eye on the performance criteria which you agreed with your appraiser and checking from time to time that the appraiser has been happy with your progress. Maybe an unforeseen difficulty developed and you talked it through with your appraiser and sought his or her help and understanding. Maybe a problem developed at home, the pressure of which led you to agree with your appraiser that your lowest priority targets would be postponed to another year. Possibly you can see that one of your remaining targets will not be achieved and the reason lies in the general pressure of other work at school. It may even be that your appraiser, as head of department, never truly delegated to you that promised responsibility agreed last year. You may feel that the fault for non-achievement lies not with you but with your appraiser's inability to use delegation effectively as a management style. The appraiser will compile his or her thoughts, too. Both should make notes to bring to the interview.

Now is the opportunity for the teacher to consider the targets he or she would like to set for the next year. What about that suggestion raised but not acted on last year, that you should chair departmental meetings for a term or two as an aspect of your development? Or that proposal you have had in mind that you lead a Baker day input on active learning in PSE? Or should one of last year's targets be reset, this time with more resources at your disposal so that you could do an even better job? Whatever the target you would like to undertake for next the year, begin to formulate it, to think of the resources necessary to achieve it and of the performance criteria which would establish its successful completion. The appraiser will also be thinking of targets which he or she would like to see achieved for the development of colleagues, the department or the school.

Years of experience of target-setting confirm that although it is a joint process, most targets are initiated by the teacher who will undertake them. They are then clarified, modified, developed, improved and agreed in conjunction with the appraiser. Sometimes those targets arise spontaneously from the appraisal discussion, but more frequently they are the result of day-to-day interaction and of careful forethought. Both parties, therefore, need to be clear about what they hope to achieve from the appraisal interview, for an unprepared participant is at a serious disadvantage in getting the best from appraisal.

4. Basic task of the teacher

Very much the same approach is needed for the basic task, except that this document is expressed in key result areas instead of as a target. The key result areas of the basic task have been identified by the school as the basic requirement of all teachers. The basic task is based on the common basic job description of all teachers at the school which in turn was extracted from the national basic task of a teacher agreed between the teacher unions and management. It is the minimum level of individual performance which is required to allow the organization to function. The key result areas of the basic task in most schools may well be similar to the following five-point plan:

1. Pastoral responsibilities
2. Teaching responsibilities
3. Personal skills development
4. Contribution to department and school community
5. Administration.

Collection of data to inform the appraisal process

Based on impressions gained during the year, the appraiser drafts out the kind of feedback that he or she believes should be given to the teacher, being careful that these impressions come from evidence, not from rumour or prejudice. The appraiser will also be sensitive to the fact that this feedback is only one side of the coin and that it must be discussed alongside the teacher's view before an agreed judgement is made. Typical sources of evidence which help both appraiser and teacher to form their judgements are:

- the professional day-to-day appraising relationship;
- developmental experiences for the teacher agreed with the appraiser;
- special support given to a colleague by the teacher;
- courses attended, qualifications gained;
- attendance, punctuality, quality of administration, etc.;
- letters or other feedback from parents;
- contributions to the running of the department or school;
- examination and attainment test results of classes;
- lesson observations.

The prospect of lesson observation causes many teachers concern, partly because of the 'unnaturalness' of having an observer at a lesson but more because of the injustice which might arise from observing a necessarily limited sample of the teacher's work. Useful guidelines for lesson observation within an appraising relationship are:

1. Encourage the relationship which develops in team teaching, where teachers watch a colleague deliver the lead lesson, discuss the aims and strategy of follow-up work, compare problems and highlights and assess together the success of the venture. That team relationship enhances all appraisal lesson observations.

2. Make lesson observation a normal feature of learning on the job. 'Could you watch me introduce this new practical work?' 'Could I watch you teach that concept: I've always found it difficult to present?' In the appraising relationship observing lessons to improve team performance is standard practice.

3. Don't let observation become all one way like judge and accused; it's a classroom not a courtroom. Both appraiser and teacher can learn from observing and being observed.

4. Have the understanding that visits to lessons can be made at any time. Check with the teacher out of courtesy and interest. Avoid elaborate and formal time fixing as if it were a duel or a dental appointment.

5. Aim to make visits to lessons so normal that neither students nor the teacher are disturbed by the visit. More can be learned about the true performance of a teacher by a dozen five-minute visits to a range of lessons than an hour's observation of a single performance.

6. Adopt a positive approach. 'Catch them doing something right' is an appropriate philosophy. After an observation, tell the teacher what you believe he or she did right and what you thought of it. Encourage the teacher to go on in the same way. If you believe something was wrong, tell the teacher. Distinguish in your reaction as appraiser between poor practice due to bad attitude and that due to lack of time, knowledge or skill.

7. Make a point of giving feedback soon after the observation. Leave as little time as possible for the teacher to be wondering what you thought of the lesson you observed.

8. Save the sustained observation of lessons for occasions when the teacher has a problem and needs the appraiser's advice; then help to identify or resolve the problem.

9. If the school system requires a formal observation, focus on a few key aspects of performance to observe and discuss. Agree them beforehand. It is impossible to observe everything which happens in a lesson and an attempt to do so leads to trivialized and superficial feedback.

10. Remember, the aim of all staff appraisal, including classroom observation, is improved performance through staff development.

Naturally this evidence of classroom performance would be presented to the teacher as it occurred, throughout the year, but at interview time the appraiser and teacher are engaged on a summarizing process. In the main they are summarizing information which would come to a teacher and a teacher's 'manager' even if there were no appraisal. If there has to be a frantic scramble for random evidence about performance, then the appraisal relationship has not worked throughout the year.

As appraiser, try to collate this information so that you have a summary of the teacher's performance over the year seen from your viewpoint. Prepare to celebrate outstanding performance and to give full credit for achievements, even if those achievements were only to perform the basic task satisfactorily. Select examples of certain types of activity to illustrate your comments Prepare in just the same way for aspects of performance which you feel are unsatisfactory, again with examples. Aim to be able to present a balanced view of the performance as you have seen it, or as illustrated by evidence to which you have access. But, having done all this preparation, the cardinal sin would be to believe that this is the only or even the most accurate view of the performance under discussion.

Unless the teacher wishes to sit passively through an appraisal interview or is happy to limit his or her contribution to reacting to the comments of the appraiser, there is a similar exercise to be undertaken by the teacher. As the teacher in the appraisal interview, are there aspects of your performance that you wish to draw to the attention of the appraiser or to have discussed? Consider this as you, the teacher, complete the performance awareness document and expect to have the matter discussed at the appraisal review.

Another important aid to the appraisal of the basic task is a copy of the agreed appraisal of that task from the previous year. Which features were highlighted a year ago as agreed strengths and weaknesses? Have the strengths remained and was there effort from the teacher and support from the appraiser in eroding the weaknesses? Again, both parties should note the thoughts which they might want to raise at the interview.

Warden Park School
Performance Awareness and Self-Appraisal Document

1. OVERALL CAREER PLAN
    (i)   What are your short and long term career plans?
    (ii) Is there any special coaching you would like from anyone on the staff?
2. REVIEW OF THE PAST YEAR
    A.   The positive aspect of the past 12 months.
        (i)   What kinds of work experiences have given you the greatest satisfaction over the past year?

(ii) Have any classes or pupils been particularly rewarding?

(iii) Has anyone in particular on the staff been of special help this year?

(iv) Which forms of training or courses of further education have you undertaken this year? (Remember to consider departmental training within your department or house as well as external courses).

B. The negative aspect of the past 12 months.

(i) What do you dislike doing that you must do in your present job?

(ii) Have any tasks been especially difficult this year?

(iii) Have any classes or pupils not been satisfactorily dealt with?

(iv) Which of your skills and talents are most under-used?

(v) What aspects needs strengthening of your technical competence managerial competence personal relationship etc.

(vi) Would you wish to attend courses on these? Or how else do you propose to gain the necessary experience and improvement?

3. GENERAL

(i) Do you have any positive comments to make about the school?

(ii) Do you have any suggestions for improving the school?

(iii) Are there any general coments you wish to make about any matter affecting your teaching performance?

(iv) Do you have an up to date job description? Do you feel that you understand all the requirements of your task?

(v) Are you satisfied with the opportunities you have to discuss your problems, your targets and your work in general?

Self-Appraisal/Interview Preparation Form

As part of the annual cycle of teacher performance appraisal you will be able to have a discussion with your head teacher/appraiser about your work during this academic year and your work plan for the coming year. The purpose of this process is to identify needs for the professional growth of all teachers and to promote teacher effectiveness by endeavouring to meet these needs wherever possible.

You may find it helpful to prepare yourself by answering these questions in advance of the interview although you are not required to make the completed form available to your appraiser if you prefer not to do so.

1. Write down what you think are the main tasks and responsibilities of your current post.

2. During the past academic year, what parts of your job have given you greatest satisfaction? How could these be used to best advantage?
3. What parts of your job have given you least satisfaction? Is there something that could be done to overcome this?
3. Were there any problems or difficulties which prevented you from achieving something you intended or hoped to do? Are they still a cause for concern? If so, could they be eliminated?
5. To help improve your performance in your job, what changes in the school organization would be beneficial?
6. What additional things might be done by your head teacher? Your head of department? You? Anyone else?
7. What do you think should be your main target(s)/goals for next year?
8. How would you like to see your career developing?

Annex B to the report of the Appraisal/Training working group of the ACAS (Advisory Conciliation and Arbitration Service) independent panel, June 1986.

29
PREPARATION OF THE PHYSICAL ENVIRONMENT

An agreed agenda?

Remember to give the teacher ample notice of the approaching review of performance. Remind him or her during the year that the basic task and the targets you set for the previous year have an agreed month for annual review. As that month approaches agree a date, time and location two or three weeks ahead for the interview. At that time issue the 'performance awareness' document, a basic task sheet and a blank target setting sheet. These are the documents which form the basis of the appraisal. In my experience, the agenda is always:

- Basic task
- Targets
- Performance awareness document.

The order of discussion is usually left to the teacher. In 15 years of schoolteacher performance appraisal at no stage did I find it necessary to hold an 'agenda-setting' meeting prior to the appraisal. However, some schools in the National Teacher Appraisal Pilot Study used such a device and found it was reassuring to teachers inexperienced in appraisal to be aware beforehand of the agreed topics. With experienced teachers, I find that working through the three documents which are central to the system does, in itself, constitute an agenda. If a previously agreed agenda seems likely to produce a more satisfactory interview then it is prudent to use it.

Schools with which I have worked as a consultant have found the chief disadvantages of an agenda-setting meeting to be:

1. The indication that one of the participants would like an issue raised frequently leads to discussion. However well this discussion is developing, it usually has to be cut short because of lack of time or lack of preparedness of the other party.
2. An appraisal meeting with a fixed agenda sometimes inhibits discussion ranging over topics which were not originally nominated.
3. The fixed agenda probably indicates key problem areas. Because of this, the interviewing process is much more likely to begin with problems and problem areas, rather than a balanced view of total performance. If it does the interview is probably getting off on the wrong foot.

Whether there is an agenda limited to nominated aspects of performance or it is agreed that the whole of the teacher's performance is under discussion based on the above three key documents, the same important guideline of 'no surprises' applies to all appraisal interviewing. Why wait until the appraisal interview to tell a teacher that he or she has, in your opinion, been effective in some aspect of performance? Certainly no negative aspect of a teacher's performance which has not been previously raised should be brought into a well-managed appraisal interview. Imagine being told at interview by your appraiser that 'I have been concerned for several months about your lateness to lessons' or 'The quality of your administration has slipped badly this year', without any indication of dissatisfaction from the appraiser at the time. 'Why didn't you tell me at the time?' the teacher will ask, while the appraiser wonders what happened to the essential appraising relationship.

The teacher spends his or her preparation time on the same exercise – considering the year's performance, identifying strengths and weaknesses, selecting examples to illustrate proposed comments. The most accurate and fairest appraisal of the previous year's performance will result if these two views are collated in the appraisal interview.

Room preparation

Now that the research preparation is completed, two other aspects of preparation remain – attitude to the interview and a check on the physical environment in which it will take place. The latter reminds us of the need to prepare an interview room, and much has been written on this theme. I offer these guidelines:

1. Isolate the interview from interruption. Making appraisal time sacred in this way

- reinforces to the teacher that the appraiser values on the occasion;
- gives confidence that the climate created for the interview will not be shattered;
- avoids the embarrassment of an intrusion into the appraisal room at a critical time, such as when the teacher is disclosing on a long-buried personal issue;
- encourages appraiser and teacher to focus on the matter in hand.

If there is to be an interruption of the discussion, let it be initiated from within the room, for example so that both participants can have a break from an intense discussion for a cup of coffee!

2. Create the environment which is most likely to relax, make comfortable and best suit the teacher. Discussions of room arrangement debate the value of easy or upright chairs, the position of the desk as a barrier or a shared facility, the location of the furniture in relation to the window, etc. Such refinements stimulate a wry smile from most teachers who know the limited resources with which they operate. In my view it would be preferable to conduct the appraisal interview in surroundings in which the teacher feels relaxed, than to create theoretically correct conditions which seem to the teacher to be stilted and artificial. How does the appraiser normally operate when the teacher wants a few words in private? Maybe those are the familiar conditions which would best suit the appraisal interview.

3. Use chairs of the same height. Mixed chair heights do nothing to reinforce the feeling of participation which needs to be created.

4. Make the desk an aid not a barrier. A desk becomes a barrier not only when it is between the participants but when the appraiser claims it as his or her territory. It is better not to use a desk at all than to use it to put the teacher at a disadvantage. Considering the number of essential documents, the need for space for note-taking and the aim to foster an open discussion between professionals, using the desk as a shared facility on which both participants can 'lay their cards on the table' is by far the best technique.

5. Place the chairs at a natural angle to each other for conversation. Watch how people sit during a normal conversation. Few of us choose to sit 'eyeball to eyeball', even fewer of us choose to sit 'ear to ear'. Most of us converse at an angle between the two which is almost 'face to face', but not quite. But be prepared for the chair to be moved before or during the interview.

6. Consider where to sit in relation to the window. Do you really want to appear in silhouette? How distracting will it be to have a view from your window of 4D in a science lesson? A strong light in the eyes might be a familiar technique to the Los Angeles police, but did you intend to use it in your office?

30
ATTITUDE PREPARATION

The attitude of the teacher

Performance appraisal is a day-to-day relationship. This is acknowledged elsewhere in this book, but the summarizing and target-setting process which represents the appraisal interview is usually an annual meeting. From the teacher's viewpoint it is 'our one big chat of the year with me and my contribution here as the centre of discussion'. What is the teacher likely to expect from the interview? Most teachers would say 'At an appraisal interview I expect to . . .'.

- state my own views on
  - my progress,
  - my future,
  - my training,
  - our department,
  - our school,
  and to be heard fairly and to discuss those views;
- listen to and discuss my appraiser's views, to be free to agree or disagree and if I disagree to be free to explain why;
- receive praise for work well done;
- be made aware of deficiencies in my performance and to have help in overcoming them;
- criticize my own performance and indicate impediments to my development, even if the impediment is my appraiser;
- have my views about my future development considered alongside the training and development plans of the school.

The importance of teacher assertiveness

A successful interview requires the teacher to be relaxed, confident and assertive. Assertiveness can be distinguished from aggression and passivity by its behaviours. With passive behaviour, needs and wants are taken care of by manoeuvring and manipulating others to take care of them. The alternative is to suppress the need. If you as a teacher are passive, then typical interview behaviours will be:

You do
- hope that you will get what you want;
- bottle up and hide your feelings;
- hope others will see your side of the story as well as theirs;
- rely on others to work out what you want by intuition;
- often play the martyr role.

You don't
- contribute your viewpoint to the interview;
- ask for what you want;
- express your feelings;
- upset anyone;
- get what you want.

In short, your passivity may result in some needs being met, but more often results in sacrificing needs, getting them met in inappropriate ways and the loss of identity and of the ability to take care of your own development.

With aggressive behaviour, needs and wants are taken care of in a forceful and self-serving way. If your attitude is aggressive, typical interview behaviours will be:

You do
- try any form of pressure to get your own way;
- threaten, manipulate, cajole, be sarcastic and quarrel;
- stir up antipathy in others.

You don't
- respect that others have a right to have their needs met;
- look for situations where all parties gain.

In short, your aggressive behaviour may accomplish your personal desires and goals but it tends to alienate people, create distrust and tension and undermine the ability to establish lasting and healthy relationships.

Clearly, if appraisal is to work to mutual benefit, the attitude to be encouraged in appraisees is one of assertiveness. With assertive behaviour, needs and wants are taken care of by knowing, accepting and acting on them in constructive, straightforward and authentic ways. Typical interview behaviours will then be:

You express your viewpoint confidently, without undue anxiety; explain what you would like to happen – directly, openly and appropriately; have rights and expect them to be respected.

You don't violate other people's rights; expect the appraiser to know by magic what you want; freeze up with anxiety.

In short, you are able to know and take care of needs in a constructive way without doing so at the expense of others.

The attitude of the appraiser

The final form of preparation requires the appraiser to appreciate that he or she is facing one of the most important meetings of the year. As a result of a successful interview the organization could have a teacher who feels that he or she matters to the school, that people at the school listen and care, and that, whether or not the teacher is seeking promotion, he or she is being helped to develop personally and professionally. The attitude required of the appraiser is one which allows the use of all his or her interview skills to draw the best from the teacher. At the same time the appraiser must demonstrate interest and respect, so that targets can be agreed which develop the teacher and simultaneously match the corporate objectives of the school.

The appraiser can develop an appropriate attitude by putting into practice certain behaviours. These behaviours are expressed in detail as skills in Chapters 31–35. In summary, an appropriate attitude can be developed by following these guidelines:

- Show respect for the teacher. Give him or her your total attention.
- Be assertive rather than aggressive or passive. Don't parade your authority or experience.
- Be aware of your personal bias. Control it by acting on evidence.
- Give feedback sensitively, in a form the teacher can handle.
- Create an atmosphere of trust in which the teacher feels safe to present and discuss his or her point of view.
- Use all the listening skills. Don't allow the interview to degenerate into an argument.
- Use the questioning skills to clarify and develop the interview.
- Use the target-setting skills to develop mutually agreed, high targets.
- Ensure that what you have agreed to be confidential remains confidential.

31
THE FIRST KEY APPRAISAL
INTERVIEW SKILL – GIVING
FEEDBACK

The importance of shared knowledge

Just as the essential spirit of the appraising school is its openness in relationships, so the same quality is the foundation of successful appraisal interviewing. The simple model shown in Figure 7, represents a teacher's total personality. By definition, knowledge about the personality can be divided as shown.

This simple analysis illustrated in Figure 7 reminds us that some of our actions and attitudes are known to us and some are not. At the same time some of our actions and attitudes are known to others and some are not. For teacher and appraiser to understand each other, for them to work on problems together, as much job-relevant knowledge as possible needs to be brought into the area of shared knowledge. It is not possible to work on a problem together if one of the participants does not know that a problem exists.

The area of shared knowledge is enhanced in practice by inputs from adjoining areas – the knowledge to which the teacher is blind and the area of private knowledge. This book is not concerned with calling up knowledge from the subconscious. Typical of the knowledge which an appraiser might hold in that 'blind' area is his or her appreciation of an observed lesson, an admiration for the way the teacher dealt with a distressed child

KNOWN TO
THE TEACHER

UNKNOWN TO
THE
TEACHER

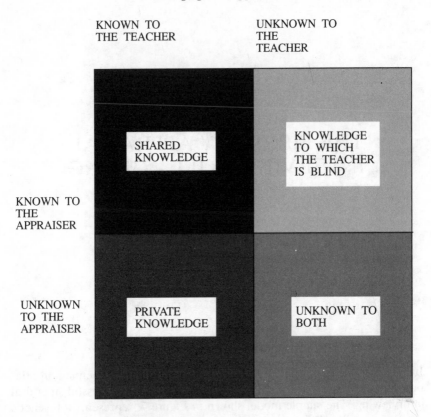

KNOWN TO
THE
APPRAISER

UNKNOWN
TO THE
APPRAISER

SHARED
KNOWLEDGE

KNOWLEDGE
TO WHICH
THE TEACHER
IS BLIND

PRIVATE
KNOWLEDGE

UNKNOWN TO
BOTH

Figure 7   Teacher's total personality.

or a positive comment on the teacher which the appraiser has received. Passing such positive information into the area of shared knowledge enhances the appraising relationship.

Passing knowledge of a problem into the area of shared knowledge means it can be worked on and this too enhances the relationship. On the other hand, an erroneous perception of a teacher which is retained by an appraiser in the area to which the teacher is blind, will not only fail to be rectified, but can influence the appraiser's judgement without the teacher being able to take any corrective action. If brought skilfully into the public area this perception can be discussed and corrected before it has time to prejudice the opinions and behaviour of the appraiser. The process of reducing the blind area and consequently enlarging the public area is, of course, the skilled technique of giving feedback.

How to give feedback

In order to be effective, feedback has to be given in a quantity and a form which the receiver can handle. Guidelines for giving feedback effectively are:

1. Give feedback soon. It is a mistake to bottle up feedback; give it as soon as you have it. This not only stops the teacher wondering whether some action was right or wrong in the appraiser's eyes, but feedback can be such a boost to morale. Too often an opportunity for positive feedback on a lesson, a report, the handling of a pupil incident or on support given to a colleague is lost because appraisers are not in the habit of giving a brief but timely acknowledgement. Even negative feedback reassures the teacher that the appraiser cares and is in touch. Also, a wrong behaviour is much easier to change before it becomes a habit.

2. Focus on behaviour. You are concerned with what people do, not with what they are. When a school employs a teacher it does not buy the right to appraise all of that teacher's personality and attributes all of the time. The school has, in effect, bought a performance from the teacher. It is on that performance that the school has the right and the duty to give feedback. The appraiser may consider the teacher to be lazy and selfish, but unless these characteristics prevent the teacher from giving a satisfactory performance, they are not prime subjects for feedback. Whatever the appraiser feels about the teacher's characteristics and lifestyle, if the teacher performs well then he or she expects positive feedback on performance.

One way of testing out whether you as appraiser are focusing on what people do, rather than what they are, is to use the illustration test. Can you illustrate the point you want to make by describing an incident or presenting some evidence of the behaviour? By remembering the 'no surprises' rule for appraisal interviewing, your illustration will be something of which the teacher is also aware. Thus you have common ground for a positive discussion.

3. Be specific not global; be descriptive not evaluative. We have just made the case for feedback being based on specific instances. Now we add the warning to present the teacher with the facts, not an evaluation of them. Appraisal aims to remove hasty, unjust judgements, not to foster them. The feedback 'You are a hopeless timekeeper' does not exactly put the teacher in the mood to discuss the matter rationally. The less global and non-evaluative statement, 'You have been late for school three time this week, on Monday, Tuesday and now again on Friday', is much more likely to provoke an explanation than the earlier feedback. In addition, of course,

the teacher who is conscientious about time but whose personal domestic problems have made lateness unavoidable in recent weeks, will rightly feel the injustice of global, evaluative feedback.

4. Avoid cosmic judgements: present the evidence rather than your judgement on it.

```
        /\
       /  \
      /SOCCER\
     /  IS A   \
    /  KICK IN   \
   / IN THE GRASS \
  /_____\
```

If you initially read the above without noticing the extra 'in', you will readily appreciate the folly of believing one's own judgements to be always correct.

A feature of appraisal skills training courses is the frequency with which participants in simulated interviews begin their feedback with 'You are . . .'. On studying the replayed videos most are embarrassed that they did not preface their remark with 'In my opinion . . .' or 'There is some evidence . . .' or some other indication of the humility of the appraiser who lacks omniscience. But there is a much more fundamental error of attitude here. An appraisal interview is a discussion of a performance from various – at least two – viewpoints. Suppose you and I are seated on opposite sides of a table on which stands a huge jug. I describe it to you by saying, 'From my viewpoint it is a large unglazed earthenware container with a sturdy handle'. You reply, 'I agree that it seems to be a large unglazed earthenware container. I did not know about the handle, because it can't be seen from here, but I can tell you that there is an indentation, a pouring lip, on the rim on this side.' Between us we have a pretty good description of the object, but if either of us had proceeded alone our understanding of what we were looking at would have been unnecessarily incorrect. If we want to use that jug to best effect we need both perceptions of it.

An exact parallel can be drawn with appraiser and teacher trying to build an accurate perception of the teacher's performance. Appraisal interviewing will not achieve its purpose if the teacher becomes accustomed to listening passively to the appraiser presenting the annual judgement of the organization on his or her performance. The teacher's own opinion must help to inform that judgement.

5. Own the feedback. Appraisal interview feedback must rise well above staffroom gossip. Much gossip begins in the third-person plural. 'They say she has . . .', without being too specific about who 'they' are. There could

be no greater contrast with appraisal feedback. The whole process has to be open and owned. Consequently, much appraisal feedback begins with 'I saw', 'I have received these three letters of congratulation' or 'In my professional judgement . . .'. With all feedback, be willing to disclose its source, whether or not that source is yourself. Only a year of experience by the Schoolteacher Appraisal Pilot authorities led them to include this warning in their code of practice: 'Any information received anonymously should not be used'. I would go much further. If you feel you cannot reveal the name of your source of information, then do not use it. If you want an open system, there can be no hidden sources. Own the feedback.

6. Think what your feedback to the teacher says about you as appraiser. You choose the areas on which to give feedback, you decide how sensitively it will be given, you decide on its quantity and its quality. Unavoidably, in presenting feedback to the teacher, you disclose much of your own skill, your own professionalism and your own values. Like it or not, appraisal interviewing is a two-way process.

32
THE SECOND KEY APPRAISAL INTERVIEW SKILL – CLIMATE CREATION FOR DISCLOSURE FROM THE TEACHER

The teacher's doubts about disclosure

We saw earlier how the 'shared' area of knowledge common to both teacher and appraiser can be enlarged by the appraiser giving feedback from the area to which the teacher is blind (see page 198). The diagram shown in Figure 7 also illustrates the fact that the shared area can be enlarged by an input from the area of private knowledge which is known only to the teacher. The decision whether to share this information with the appraiser clearly rests with the teacher, since only the teacher knows of its existence. If in doubt about this, the teacher may reflect in this way:

- Is it appropriate and relevant to the appraisal?
- Do I feel comfortable with the likely reaction of the appraiser?
- Will I be given enough time to explain the matter in full?
- Will it prejudice the appraiser's view of me?
- Do I need to disclose it? Is it better kept to myself?
- Is the appraiser a worthy and sensitive person with whom to discuss this matter?

What kind of information might the teacher have which could help the appraisal if it were disclosed? Obviously the appraisal process needs the teacher's view of the 'jug', namely his or her own performance in the school. But the quality of interaction might be improved if the teacher felt confident to discuss his or her professional hopes, fears, frustrations and shortcomings. Until the teacher explains his or her feelings on an issue, the appraiser is left to act on assumptions – a dangerous practice. How many times has tiredness been mistaken for lack of interest in the job? Or shyness assumed to be lack of confidence? Or modesty to be lack of ambition? What are the dangers for the appraiser who assumes that every effective teacher must want promotion or that part-time teachers are not committed to the job as full-time teachers? The danger of assumption on any matter can be avoided if the teacher chooses to tell the appraiser of his or her feelings on the matter.

How to create the right climate

The decision on whether this information is to become shared knowledge will always rest with the teacher, but some of the teacher's doubts would be eased if the appraiser could create the right conditions for disclosure. Making the climate right between the two participants is encouraged in the following way:

1. Set an atmosphere of trust. This cannot be done by the head announcing to the staff in Friday's staff meeting 'As from 9 o'clock on Monday there will be trust, understanding and honesty between us here at Goathill'. Trust is built and nurtured by day-to-day contact between teacher and appraiser. For example, I decide as a teacher to tell you, my appraiser, of a work-related problem which has been troubling me for some time and ask you to help and to discuss it with me in confidence. If next day I find that half of the staff are talking about a matter that I was desperate to keep confidential between us, then trust is shattered. If, on the other hand, I find that you privately help, advise and support me through my difficulty, then I would, with much less anxiety, discuss matters with you in future. Trust between us is growing. Trust can only be nurtured and developed; it cannot be achieved by decree.

Trust can be confirmed and encouraged in the appraisal interview by:

- empathizing with the teacher's problems and concerns;
- showing understanding of the teacher's self-disclosure remarks rather than judging them;
- ensuring that full, but genuine praise is given for achievements;
- being willing, as appraiser, to disclose some matter in your own teaching performance, especially if it relates to a similar experience;
- not flaunting any kind of authority.

2. Set a participative atmosphere. There is more likely to be appropriate disclosure if the teacher is aware that an appraisal interview is a vehicle for two-way communication; it allows the interchange of information so that appropriate courses of action can be decided on. Do this by creating space in the interview for the teacher to do the talking. Effective questioning and listening techniques to achieve this are discussed later (see Chapters 33 and 34). Give the teacher your whole attention and make it evident that you are doing so.

3. Seek only organizationally relevant information. Any suggestion of snooping, meddling or voyeurism will stand out as such. There is a marked difference between the above, and seeking to create an atmosphere in which it is comfortable for a teacher to relax and discuss professional performance openly and frankly. Give attention to issues of confidentiality and obtain agreement about the circumstances in which you can discuss them outside the interview room.

4. Develop the maturity to accept feedback. Years of practice in not receiving feedback have made feedback difficult for us to accept. Positive, favourable feedback on our performance makes us embarrassed and diffident. We try to explain away our success, our diligence or our skills. We say 'It was nothing' or we try to give the credit to someone else even when it is rightfully ours. It is rare to find a teacher willing to accept positive feedback as a right because it fits into the teacher's own objective assessment of his or her contribution to the school.

In just the same way only those teachers or appraisers with high maturity can take negative feedback on performance. Yet it is not rare in the search for obstacles to improved teacher performance to find that one of those blockages is the performance of the appraiser as head of a department or other form of teacher manager. Appraisers need this feedback from their staff to develop and improve their own performance. If the appraiser chokes it off, valuable perspective on him or herself is lost. In future, the teacher will avoid commenting, will pretend or will play games rather than upset an appraiser who is too immature to take feedback on his or her own development.

A more fruitful action on being given negative feedback on performance is to stay calm and to clarify the feedback. Ask the person providing the feedback what alternative behaviour he or she would prefer to see happening in your performance. Then take time to think about the accuracy of the feedback and the value of changed behaviour.

33
THE THIRD KEY APPRAISAL INTERVIEW SKILL – ACTIVE LISTENING

The effects of good and bad listening

Pressure of time has made listening a lost art in schools. If you doubt this, watch teachers as they talk to each other in staffrooms and corridors. We interrupt each other, make assumptions about what was meant and even finish each other's sentences. For a successful appraisal interview, listening skills have to be revived. Good listening emphasizes:

- respect for the teacher;
- that the contribution of the teacher matters to the appraiser;
- that the appraiser wants to help in ways which matter to the teacher;
- that appraisal is not a 'tell' situation.

We have said that a good balance of talk in an appraisal interview is 70 per cent from the teacher and 30 per cent from the appraiser. The balance of listening is, therefore, the reverse of these ratios.

What is the effect on the teacher of the appraiser not listening? Feedback from those who have experienced talking to someone who exhibits all the signs of not listening, confirms that the common reactions can include any of the following:

- anger and indignation;

- loss of confidence, anxiety, loss of concentration and the feeling that the speaker is somehow to blame for the unsatisfactory interview;
- a tendency to give up, cut the meeting short and stifle any intended disclosure.

Listening is an active not a passive process. Good listening means more than just hearing the spoken words; it means thinking about them, the way in which they were said and about their significance and implication. As an appraiser you must be able to listen to what the teacher is saying, to what the teacher is avoiding saying and for what the teacher cannot say without your help. How is this done?

How to develop the skills of listening

1. Make it evident that you are listening. Sit comfortably but attentively. Though it is possible to listen from a reclining position, with hands behind the head and eyes closed, it is hard to convey attention from such a pose. Sit leaning forward slightly but avoid looking like a cobra poised to strike. Aim for comfortable eye contact. Use natural acknowledgements, such as saying 'I see' or nodding your understanding occasionally, to confirm that you are still there and listening.

2. Let your listening show on your face. The interested listener shows reaction to what he or she is being told. Maintain appropriate eye contact, change facial expression at suitable times. Smile where it is opportune.

3. Stop talking. Your constant chatter is a great deterrent to the teacher who has something to say. Make spaces in the interview for the teacher's input. Use open questions to allow the teacher opportunity to raise a wide range of issues which matter to him or her.

4. When it is appropriate for you to talk, practise listening for sound clues which indicate the teacher's reaction to what you are saying – listen for the murmur, the groan, the sigh, the mutter.

5. Allow silences without embarrassment. The inexperienced appraiser often feels nervous of allowing silences and in his or her embarrassment fills the silence with talk or with a second question while the teacher is still pondering the answer to the first.

6. Avoid negative signals. These come in many forms. Evaluating what is being said while it is being said is a show-stopper. Evaluate it together later: for now just listen and understand. Another impediment to the teacher is the appraiser who, looking out of the window or at the clock, says 'Hmmm,

that's really interesting, Brian'. Try convincing Brian of your genuine concern once he has been deterred by your signalling. Other examples of negative signals are:

frustration – hand clenching or wringing, rubbing the back of the neck;
boredom – drumming the table, doodling, tapping the feet or the 'head in the palm of the hand' position;
rejection – tightly folded arms, peering over the glasses, squinting hard, turning the body away.

7. Listen for areas the teacher wants to talk about but doesn't know how to get started on. An appraiser needs to know how to look for these 'doors' to problem areas. Usually they come wrapped in other comments, such as the teacher saying to the head of department, 'We're all so busy this year in the department. I know it's hard for you to decide who to develop and support. . . . But then you're short of time like the rest of us. I'm looking forward to next year's timetable which looks really well thought out.' In a flash the lack of support and development which that teacher feels has been hinted at, rationalized and finally wrapped up in a positive comment on next year's timetable. Now is the time for the appraiser to use a door-opening technique, with a phrase such as 'You mentioned staff development in the department, would you like to talk more about that?' or 'I'd be interested to hear your views on . . .'. Good listening means listening for what the teacher cannot say without your help.

8. Listen for areas of agreement, not only for conflict areas.

9. Summarize and reflect back what you hear. This is an important technique not only to display to the teacher what you understand to have been said, but also to give the teacher an opportunity to correct or add to that message. 'So in other words, John, if I planned departmental meetings better, you would feel better prepared to contribute to them?' 'Yes, that's right Brenda, and especially if the agenda could be available a week or so ahead of the meeting.' Paraphrase at intervals throughout the interview; some of those summaries can usefully be turned into targets.

Two especially important occasions for summarizing are, first, when the appraiser feels he or she wants to reject or disagree with what the teacher is saying. Summarizing and reflecting back are ways of clarifying. Always clarify before disagreeing. Second, when the appraiser will be required to make a decision based on what has been said. In both cases, it is essential to understand what is being said and if possible the teacher's reason for saying it.

10. Reflect back feelings. A more advanced form of listening is being aware not only of the words which are said but also of the way in which they are spoken. Listen for feelings, inflection, pace. A departmental head in an appraisal interview with a deputy headteacher said, 'I applied for the post advertised internally last year for a curriculum co-ordinator but I wasn't interviewed'. Now as a statement of fact that was perfectly correct, and an appraiser might well treat it as such. But the way in which it was said in this particular case revealed such pent-up emotion, on a matter which was settled a year ago, that it was clearly affecting the performance, attitude and even the happiness of the head of department. It may, therefore, be opportune to encourage this man to talk out his feelings. The deputy headteacher thought so, and tried to reflect back the feeling and emotion which he had seen. 'John, that seems to have upset you a great deal' was all he said, but it was enough to encourage John to talk through the whole matter and dissipate a great deal of bitterness and reverse a deteriorating performance.

34
THE FOURTH KEY APPRAISAL INTERVIEW SKILL – ASKING QUESTIONS

Types of question

Although interviews are aware that a practical guide to the balance of talking in an appraisal interview is about 70:30 in favour of the appraisee, many disappoint themselves with an excessive amount of talking. In analysing their interviews afterwards they attribute their desire to talk to a need they feel not to lose control of the interview. True, the appraiser does have an obligation of control, but control is not judged on the balance of talking. Control is judged on achieving purposes, raising prepared points and gaining planned insights. The most effective technique for controlling the interview, while leaving the balance of talking with the teacher is to develop effective questioning skills.

The simplest and most widely accepted classification of questions is into open and closed questions, but the analysis can be widened to help in the development of an appropriate technique. There is no suggestion that one of these types of questioning is good and another bad. Each has its particular uses.

Closed questions

Closed questions seek specific items of information, for example 'Was the report written by you or by Kevin?' Usually the question seeks such a specific piece of information that a one-word answer will suffice, most often 'yes' or 'no', for example 'Will you be ready to make the presentation on Thursday?' Elementary as this may appear, I have witnessed many an interview fail because the appraiser persists in asking closed questions while the frustrated teacher is criticized for failing to open up in the interview. This is the appropriate tool to gain an answer to a specific question but an inappropriate tool to open up a discussion.

Open questions

Open questions are intended to allow the teacher to be expansive, to give scope for putting up a wide range of ideas, emotions or attitudes. The question from the appraiser 'Would you tell me about the first of the targets we agreed last year?' allows the teacher to select the form of his or her reply. He or she could describe it, recount how it was achieved, identify the problems encountered, analyse the feelings from frustration to elation which came as the target project developed.

Appraisers sometimes find it frustrating that the answer does not provide them with the information they expected. In practice the teacher is likely to raise those matters which most concern him or her about the target. In order to discover the information he or she is seeking, the appraiser may need to follow this initial open question with a balanced sequence of closed questions or questions of other types.

The possible lack of specificity in questions and answers in an interview which was run entirely on open questions might leave both participants with a feeling of wading through treacle. However, open questions are a powerful aid in setting the participative tone required in an interview. The successful interview is a discussion of a teacher's performance in a relaxed participative mode. As appraiser you already know how you see that performance and can present that to the teacher. What you need now is an opportunity to obtain the opinions, feelings and facts to which the teacher has access, in other words the teacher's view of the job and the future. To achieve, this try asking open questions which begin in this way:

- 'What have been the most . . . ?'
- 'How do you feel you did . . . ?'
- 'What forms of training do you need for . . . ?'
- 'Which aspects of your job . . . ?'
- 'How have you found dealing with . . . ?'
- 'What priorities do you see . . . ?'
- 'Where do you see yourself . . . ?'

Clarifying questions

Clarifying questions can be open or closed in form, but need to be identified as a means of helping a teacher to convey exactly what he or she wants to say. 'Could you be more precise about the forms of support which would help you most?' 'Can you help me to understand how you feel when I formally observe your practical lessons?' 'What do you want me to understand by your phrase "a threatening experience"?' Clarifying needs to be carried out sensitively; a barrage of aggressive probing liberally spread with such phrases as 'What do you mean, you need help?' soon becomes an interrogation.

Reflective questions

Reflective questioning is a simple, but little used technique which, if used sparingly, is almost invariably effective. It involves reflecting back to the teacher the phrase he or she has just used. The effect on the teacher is to explain or expand on that remark. 'You say you have been unhappy in the department this term?' Sometimes reflecting as little as a single word will act as the trigger for expansion, for example 'Unhappy?'

Reflecting can be achieved either by repeating the actual words of the teacher or by rephrasing them. In a difficult or volatile situation, it is unwise to rephrase; better to repeat the actual words. There are probably enough sparks flying over the tinder already without risking the reply 'That's not what I said. You're putting words into my mouth!'

Use this technique selectively to keep the dialogue on the same point and to show interest without showing bias. If over-used, it can turn an interview into a farce.

Hypothetical questions

Hypothetical questioning is a technique for sounding out reaction, exploring possibilities and testing attitude. 'If you were given a temporary promotion, what would your priorities be?' Frequently used in selection interviewing, it can also help an appraiser to illustrate projected difficulties and can help a teacher to make a constructive contribution to departmental management. It is an excellent device to use in a participative style in teacher development, allowing the teacher to explore possibilities before taking action. Hypothetical questioning can backfire, if, in an appraisal interview it is not made abundantly clear that the promotion under discussion is entirely hypothetical and is in no way a hint, a proposal or, even less, a promise.

Summarizing questions

Summarizing questions are used to offer the appraiser's summary to the teacher for approval and agreement. 'So is what you are saying that this has been a very satisfying year in general, but pressure of time prevented you from making as great a success of the trial assessment programme as you would have liked?' Since it is essential that the interview does not proceed on a series of misunderstandings, this technique is useful to check the appraiser's perception and to give the teacher the opportunity to correct or add to the summary. Presenting it as a question removes the risk of the appraiser's summary appearing to be an irrefutable statement which 'may be taken down and used in evidence'.

There are, however, two types of questioning which almost invariably prove to be counter-productive in appraisal interviewing: leading questions and multiple questions.

Leading questions

Leading questions have few safe uses. 'I expect you feel, as I do, that sound preparation for attainment testing is our top priority in the next few months, don't you?' The question is so loaded and so full of pressure that it could only be asked tongue in cheek. It is wise to respect teachers sufficiently not to tell them what they feel, think or want. Let them tell you. Leading questions have no serious place in appraisal interviewing.

Multiple questions

Multiple questioning is another bad interviewing habit. The teacher is unsure which of the questions to answer and may quite sensibly pick the easiest. Often such strings of questions carry the answer to one question in the question which follows. 'Where do you expect to be in three years' time? Do you think you will be promoted? What will happen to your role in our five-year plan if you leave?' Ask a single question, listen to the answer and let it determine the phrasing of your next question.

How to use your questions in a sequence

A balance of types of question is necessary in an appraisal interview. Too many closed questions result in a frustrating interrogation for the teacher. Too many open questions leave the interview with an unclear direction. Too many clarifying or reflective questions result in the interview going round in circles. Too much summarizing leads to painfully slow progress. With too many hypothetical questions, we seem to have left the real world behind.

In addition to using a range of questions, appraisers should be prepared to use a sequence of questions in order to reach a planned point. Unplanned random questioning can look as if the appraiser is more interested in asking questions than in hearing answers. However, it is wise to strike a balance between planning a series of questions and phrasing your next question in response to the teacher's last answer. The point of balance comes with having a good series of open questions ready on key interview topics and, on the other hand, remaining interested and alert enough to use other forms of questioning to get precise information, to clarify, to summarize, etc. Follow your initial open question with an appropriate other types of question, depending on the answer given by the teacher. For example:

Appraiser: What do you feel about the relevance of the targets the department achieved last year to your work in the department this year Ann?

OPEN QUESTION

Teacher: Well, Brian, the targets were all relevant to the year in which they were achieved, but I feel sure that one in particular has had far-reaching effects on our work this year – the setting up of these appraisal interviews.

Appraiser: How have they affected your work in the department? (Repeated, now that we are clear which target the teacher has selected as important.)

OPEN QUESTION

Teacher: I feel much more involved.

Appraiser: Involved?

REFLECTIVE QUESTION

Teacher: Yes, I seem to matter, now. Also, we know where we're heading in the department and I can see more clearly my job in relation to the others.

Appraiser: What do you mean when you say that you 'seem to matter now'?

CLARIFYING QUESTION

Teacher: No I shouldn't have said that. I've always known that I matter as a person here.

(Long pause while the teacher reflects on what she has said and tries to select phrases to illustrate her point better. The appraiser is sufficiently confident to wait through the silence. Had he rushed to fill the silence he would have missed a valuable perspective on the new system.)

Well, I suppose what I really mean is that my opinion matters now. I know it does because you are asking for it this year. Just like you're doing now really. And you quote me and the others in our meetings.

Appraiser: Are you satisfied with the system?

CLOSED QUESTION

Teacher: No, not completely, Brian.

Appraiser: OK then, Ann. Help me with this one. If you were in my position, how
would you improve it?   HYPOTHETICAL QUESTION

In all appraisal questioning, allow the teacher time to think through and
phrase his or her answer. Be sure the answer is finished before continuing.
Allowing time in this way encourages a more relaxed interview, but the confidence to take the time comes from the way the appraiser is managing the
interview. Asking questions may seem an elementary skill but it is the essence,
not only of moving the interview forward, but of controlling and relaxing it as
well.

35
THE FIFTH KEY APPRAISAL INTERVIEW SKILL – TARGET-SETTING

Gains from target-setting

The role of target-setting in the appraising school has been discussed earlier (see page 41); here we concentrate on its role in the appraisal process and the appraisal interview.

If the basic task of a teacher can be described as the minimum level of performance which the organization can accept, a target is one special task raised to a high priority for achievement within a set period. It is usually an aspect of performance over and above the basic task; it represents a kind of 'credit' which a teacher may choose to aim for. For many teachers, undertaking a target will not mean doing any additional work because they regularly perform tasks in excess of what the school could demand of them. The formality of target-setting

- gives the teacher recognition for the achievement of additional work;
- ensures that any target a teacher undertakes meets an individual or an organizational need which can be co-ordinated and directed;
- ensures the best use of teacher time and of other scarce resources;
- allows targets to be used as part of planned staff development;
- implies that the school gives approval, support and resources for the target.

The role of target-setting in the appraisal interview is to make plans for development and improvement, following the successful use of the other four skills – giving feedback, creating a disclosing climate, listening and questioning. Without effective target-setting, the appraisal interview may well be a useful exchange of views, but there will be no agreement on how performance or conditions will change in the future.

During the interview, the skill of summarizing is used by the appraiser to draw together the most important points. Often these points require action and the best form of planned action is as a target. Sometimes the appraiser will prefer to complete a discussion of the teacher's accomplishments and concerns and will turn attention only at the end of the interview to the setting of targets. At other times it may seem more appropriate to set targets throughout the interview following each summary, while the issue is still warm. The proposed targets would then be drawn together at the end of the interview so that it could be decided which of them the teacher would take up.

The role of the appraiser in target-setting

In a participative interview, as the appraisal interview should be, the role of the appraiser is as a facilitator, helping the teacher to identify appropriate target-setting areas by:

1. Acknowledging the teacher's suggestions for targets. Some of these might have been prepared beforehand by the teacher and possibly signalled on the performance awareness document. Others will have arisen in the interview room from a discussion of how the problems and concerns of the teacher might be overcome. Most suggestions for targets will have been formed through the appraising relationship – the continuous professional discussion between appraiser and teacher during the year from which the teacher has probably selected five or six as proposed targets for the year ahead.
2. Exploring those suggestions. The greater the attention which can be paid to this exploration, the more likely it is that agreed appropriate targets will emerge. Why are the targets being proposed? What form of developmental support will best ensure their achievement?
3. Discussing benefits and drawbacks of the suggestions in relation to present performance, development of the teacher's potential and the continued development of the organization.
4. Drawing out other suggestions from the teacher. It is preferable to spend time on this stage rather than move quickly to the next. Would some other developmental need form the basis of a more appropriate target? The worst impression to create is that seeking the suggestions of the teacher is a contrivance, prior to the appraiser raising and forcing other targets.

5. The appraiser offering his or her own suggestions and discussing their benefits and drawbacks. Do this as an appraiser only when the teacher has run out of ideas, preferably proposing targets in an area where it is agreed that there is still an aspect of performance which needs development. There may well be some suggestion which the appraiser would like the teacher to consider. Alternatively, there may be some departmental project which the teacher could undertake which would link personal development with departmental development.

How to set targets

Good target-setting answers the following five questions:

1. What do I have to do?
2. How will we know when I've done it?
3. How will we know how well I have done it?
4. Which target takes priority?
5. What if I can see a difficulty in achieving a target?

What do I have to do?

Define clearly what has to be achieved. Although clear exposition may be the stock-in-trade of the teacher, it is surprising how a target phrased by one participant can be misunderstood by another. We all know of the classic newspaper headlines which allow the reader to be unsure of the editor's intention: 'Incest more common than thought in USA' or 'Lesotho women make beautiful carpets'. A misunderstanding could be much less amusing for the teacher who prepares for the wrong target. The answer, of course, is to undertake the phrasing jointly in the interview, or to allow one of the participants to phrase the target but to submit it to the other before it is finally agreed. Whatever the device chosen, remember that a teacher undertaking a target is tackling an item over and above the basic task. It may involve him or her in hours of work; the least the appraiser can do is to clarify with the teacher what has to be achieved.

Be as specific about the required result, but be as flexible as the task allows on the means of achievement. Allow the teacher, as a fellow professional, some scope to develop his or her own way of working.

How will we know when I've done it?

It is important to select performance criteria on which a judgement can be made about whether or not the target has been achieved. Where the criteria can be objective, there may be little problem. For example, the target 'To improve the speed with which marked homework is returned to pupils in the department', may produce the performance criteria 'Return time to be reduced to 5 days maximum'. But many of the targets which teachers undertake require more complex professional judgements. Take, for instance, the target, proposed by a modern languages teacher for herself, to 'Improve the interest in French of year 8 classes'. Clearly, interest is going to be difficult to measure. In itself it will be a subjective, professional judgement. But on what information should that judgement be based? What objective criteria can be collected and laid before the teacher and appraiser so that they may agree that the target has been achieved?

Begin by discussing the purpose of the task, which will bring us closer to the ground we need to search for our evidence. Let us say that one purpose is for the greater interest and motivation of the pupils, another to make the teacher's task more rewarding, another to improve the quality of work in the department and another purpose is to satisfy the parents of the pupils. The performance criteria, subjective and objective, which can be spread before the appraiser and the teacher for discussion on whether or not the target with year 8 French classes is achieved, therefore, might be:

1. The opinion of the teacher. This is a valuable opinion, since the teacher was very close to the action, but many teachers under-rate their performance. In this case the teacher's opinion was that having taught a year 3 class for the past seven years, she rated this to be the most interested and motivated she had taught. However, she still did not feel that there was the level of motivation for which she had hoped. 'I feel I worked very hard on the task, but it didn't make quite the difference I had hoped for,' was the verdict of the teacher herself.

2. The pupils. It was decided to use three criteria:
   - Pupil success in internal attainment tests at the end of year 3. This class achieved better results than any previous year 3 group taught by this teacher. Both teacher and appraiser were aware that other factors could operate here, for example the efficacy of teaching prior to year 3, the fact that some of those years were disturbed by industrial action, the gradual improvement in the experience and technique of the teacher concerned, etc.
   - Percentage of pupils choosing French as an an option subject for year 4. This percentage rose from 72 per cent to 94 per cent. Again, this looks very positive, but may have been influenced by other factors, for example the increase in media coverage stressing the value of modern languages as Britain's role in Europe increases, the intention

to make languages a compulsory foundation subject, the structure of the options in relation to other subjects, etc.

- Pupil opinion survey. A simple, four-question survey had been carried out with equivalent classes during the previous year and it was decided to do the same this year and compare results. The survey showed a more positive feeling towards French than in the previous survey, but not an overwhelming love of the language. Contributory factors could have been the relationship between the teacher and the class, the accuracy of the survey, the willingness of pupils to express their feelings, etc.

Both teacher and appraiser agreed, following an examination of these factors, that the methods the teacher was using were succeeding and there seemed to be an increase in the level of interest of the pupils in learning French.

3. The opinion of parents. This was to be judged on parental reaction. It was usual to receive during year 8 between 12 and 20 letters per year (4 or 5 per class) from parents, almost all of them asking that their child give up French before the end of the year or be given some special consideration because of a dislike of the language. In this year only nine negative letters were received, none of them from the class of the target teacher. However, three letters from parents did request that their child continue with the target teacher on entering year 9. Again, other factors could have operated but on the 'parental reaction' test, the teacher seems to have succeeded.

4. The opinion of the head of department. The appraiser, as head of department, had visited the lessons briefly many times during the year and had formally observed one lesson. She herself thought the teacher's techniques were a very positive and successful development. She also took into account the reaction and interest of the department in the work and the change she felt in pupil reaction to those French lessons.

The appraiser and the teacher spent some time exploring these criteria. The teacher much appreciated the professional interest being taken in her work and, having considered all factors, agreed that the experiment was a successful one. The target, they agreed, had been met. The teacher's targets for the next year grew out of this one. First, a target was agreed of making a presentation to the department on the teaching methods used. Second, a target was agreed of using the same methods with two other classes. Incidentally, following the presentation by the teacher to the department, all members of the department set targets for themselves involving those interest-raising methods.

In a target where the final judgement was inevitably to be subjective, the teacher and appraiser had used both objective and subjective 'indicators' to inform that judgement and make it a more professional one. The whole process had bound teacher and appraiser more securely into their appraising relationship, the quality of work in the department had been improved and the teacher had gained valuable ground in personal and professional development.

How will we know how well I have done it?

Into most targets it is possible to build measurement criteria, or standards, which are agreed by both parties and will indicate degrees of success. A particular advantage for the teacher of setting such performance standards is the scope it gives for self-monitoring. The advantage for the appraiser is the prior clarification of performance levels. For example, as a head I was keen to have as many parents as possible come to the school by appointment to discuss the annual report on their child. With the pastoral deputy I would agree that over 95 per cent attendance, 5 per cent delivered and discussed at home and 0 per cent sent by post would be a very good performance. Better attendance figures would be excellent. Lower attendance figures with a corresponding increase in delivered reports would still be good, down to 90 per cent attending and 10 per cent being delivered. Achievements below these figures would not be a satisfactory performance and would need some improvement or explanation, as would any increase in reports sent by post. By using agreed and clearly understood standards, we both knew, well before the annual appraisal interview, how well the pastoral system had performed in that respect.

The parameters, which can be used to define any target and to agree on levels of performance beforehand, fall into four categories:

1. Time – meeting deadlines, regular meeting dates, completion of projects, review dates, punctuality.
2. Cost – working to budgets, reduction of costs, stock levels.
3. Quantity – examination and test pass rates, attendance rates, numbers of complaints.
4. Quality – judgement of a fellow professional, GCSE grade standards, feedback from colleagues.

For some targets, the criteria will be mainly objective; for others they will be mainly subjective. Objective criteria are those which rely mainly on actual facts, uncoloured by feelings or opinions, for example 'Reduce expenditure on ordering costs by 10 per cent by 1st May' or 'Achieve a 75 per cent pass rate by 31st September'. Subjective criteria rely mainly on a personal or individual point of view, for example 'Improve relationships with school governors by 1st January' or 'Raise the morale of the cleaning staff in the school by 31st December'. Where a judgement is a subjective one, use any available objective criteria to improve the quality of the professional subjective judgement.

Which target takes priority?

The basic task is the essential performance a school requires from its staff to be able to operate. Targets are undertaken over and above this basic, essential level of performance. One cannot compensate for shortcomings in the essential basic task by taking on optional extra work elsewhere. An example of this is the teacher who arrives late in the mornings but stays each evening to run an art club. There can be no trade-off in this way with the essentials of performance. In fact, no target should be undertaken which compromises the achievement of the basic task. Whenever targets are proposed, such as plays, field trips, industrial liaison or meetings which would take the teacher temporarily away from the basic task, agreement is needed on how that task will be fulfilled during the teacher's absence.

Even so, when teachers take on several targets it is wise to set some priority between them. Some targets, once agreed, become critical to the operation of the organization. A head of department who, in place of the deputy headteacher, agrees for reasons of personal development to produce the school timetable this year will be aware how necessary that exercise is to the school. He or she could not decide not to achieve it without serious consequences and that target would therefore be rated very highly. Systems for indicating priority should at the very least distinguish between targets which are critical and those which may be equally worthy, but are only desirable from the viewpoint of the organization.

What if I can see a difficulty in achieving a target?

When agreeing targets the appraiser has an obligation to ensure that there is mutual agreement on feasibility. Though targets are intended to be challenging, forcing targets on a teacher who believes them to be unachievable, is counter-productive. Forced targets jeopardize the relationship, are demoralizing for the teacher trying to achieve them and bottle up trouble for the future when the target is missed. In an interview where the appraiser is forcing targets, the relationship is often characterized by patronizing, insincere, pressurizing, belittling, threatening behaviour, with even a touch of blackmail. These are certainly not features on which to build a relationship.

Targets must be agreed to be achievable. Even with targets which appeared to both participants to be achievable when they were set, difficulties may arise during the year which make them unrealistic. Changes in personal conditions at home, such as the illness of a relative, may usurp the time intended for the target. Job conditions may change; for example, two teachers may leave the department and the teacher may have to unexpectedly support the work of two temporary staff for a term or more. Job priorities may change. The target to develop a new course may be overtaken by industrial action, and the target 'Maintain present courses and standards' then becomes a more important and realistic one than developing new courses. In an appraisal relationship there has to be a willingness to revise targets. Which of us would take on a target if agreeing it meant being saddled with a task without the possibility of review and amendment.

Failure to perform the basic task – a special case for target-setting

All targets above the basic task are undertaken voluntarily, but, once entered into, they are a commitment from the teacher and the organization to complete. Failure to achieve a target is a call to action to discover the reason, propose and select solutions and provide appropriate support. There is, however, one aspect of performance where this approach to target-setting is not appropriate. The basic task is the minimum level of performance which a teacher must give to enable the organization to function. Any inability to deliver that level of performance must have immediate action to

- support the teacher in such a way that the performance level is delivered, even if with assistance, so that the organization may continue to function effectively;
- set a target with the teacher to raise performance to the required level through 'planned experience', training and monitoring.

However, in an interview with a teacher who is failing to achieve the basic task, it is still necessary to use all the key appraisal techniques discussed earlier, in order to bring the teacher to an understanding of the need for a target in the deficient area. This target will have one key difference from the usual target. It will be compulsory, not voluntary. Even so, it is important to allow space for the teacher to agree the need and the target. Much of the interview may be devoted to questioning, listening, creating the climate for disclosure from the teacher and giving feedback in order to reach this understanding and set the essential target. If, finally, it is not possible to convince the teacher of the need to produce this minimum level of performance then the cause is all but lost. The target must be set anyway. It must be set by the appraiser along with all the criteria to ensure that there can be no misunderstanding about target achievement.

If the failure to perform is due to lack of willingness on the part of the teacher, then, without a change in performance level, the inevitable outcome is the commencement of one of the procedures to terminate employment. However, with the teacher who is not achieving the minimum performance level because of lack of a specific skill, he or she is usually willing to receive support and to aim to remedy the deficiency. Only if this improvement programme fails and the teacher remains totally unable to perform in some aspect of the basic task, such as to maintain discipline, to carry out assessments or to report to parents, will the unfortunate teacher be required to leave. The teacher who is perfectly able to achieve the basic task standard but refuses to do so will, of course, reach the same point in much shorter time.

The foundations of the appraising relationship are trust, understanding and honesty. These qualities are exhibited, shared and developed in large part by the way in which targets are set, revised and reviewed in the appraisal interview.

36
THE INTERVIEW

The teacher's viewpoint

For you as a teacher, the appraisal interview is your annual opportunity to plan your work for the year ahead, have your work of the past year acknowledged and reviewed, sort out work-related problems, influence the way in which you are managed and review your aims and your career plans. Your appraiser will prepare for this interview. To make the most of the opportunity you should do the same. The performance awareness document will help you with many ideas, but you need not be limited by it. Make notes of points you want to raise and of actual examples which illustrate your point. Use this checklist to help you:

1. Look at the description of the basic task of a teacher at your school. Which aspects have you carried out exceptionally well and which have been inhibited by
   - you and your own concerns,
   - your own deficiency in skills, knowledge or abilities,
   - your appraiser,
   - your colleagues in the department,
   - other departments,
   - the way the work is planned and organized,
   - any other limiting factor?
2. Look at the targets which you set for last year. To what extent do you feel they have been met? Use the list above to consider the reason for your achievements being inhibited. If you have not been able to achieve a target, be prepared to say so and to discuss it like a problem, identifying

reasons and accepting appropriate help. If you have achieved your targets, expect your appraiser to enjoy reviewing the targets and giving you the praise you deserve.

3. What training and development would lead to your improved performance? Staff development is not only for those hell bent on promotion. Staff development can aim to improve your competence, increase your interest or just make the job more enjoyable.

4. Check the date and time of the interview. Expect to be given a break before the interview so that you can compose and refresh yourself. Bring all relevant documents (including letters, certificates, etc.) and your notes to the meeting. Bring writing equipment so that you can make notes there as well as help to frame your targets for next year.

5. Expect the appraiser to seek your opinion on any aspect of your performance, especially the basic task and targets. The appraiser will also give you performance feedback. The appraiser is trained in these skills as well as in sensitive questioning and in listening. Help the appraiser to use those techniques. Without your participation the appraiser will be left with no alternative but to tell you what your appraisal is. It takes two people to make a success of an interview.

6. Consider your attitude prior to the appraisal. You need to be assertive, co-operative and participative. A balanced view of you, your performance and your development will not emerge as clearly unless you are an active partner in the appraisal interview.

The appraiser's viewpoint

At the interview, perhaps more than at any other time, your performance as appraiser, as well as that of the teacher, is under review. You are under review to see if you can be bothered as a person and as a senior representative of the school or college, to take time to prepare. You are also under review to face the facts. Without the relevant data, not only will feedback and planning be incomplete, but any shortcoming in preparation registers with the teacher as a lack of interest. 'Our one big chat of the year and he couldn't be bothered to prepare for it!' says the teacher as he or she discusses the experience with friends. In our case, however, we will have made our preparations, using this list to ensure nothing is forgotten.

Checklist for the appraiser

1. Give the teacher a written description of the system. Describe to the

teacher, in advance, the purpose of the meeting and the procedure. Make sure the teacher is aware of his or her role.

2. Give the teacher a performance awareness ('warm-up') document. Agree an agenda if necessary.
3. Fix a mutually convenient time.
4. Review and prepare interview notes on:
   - the targets set last year,
   - the key result areas of the basic task,
   - any other aspect of performance of which you have evidence and the teacher is already aware.
5. Prepare the interview room in the way most likely to put the teacher at ease.
6. Ensure there will be no interruptions.
7. Conduct your own attitude preparation, reminding yourself to use the five key appraisal skills of:
   - giving feedback – consider how to deliver the feedback you have compiled;
   - receiving feedback – plan how you will create the right atmosphere for this teacher to disclose all they want to tell you;
   - listening – concentrate on listening for what is said and what is being avoided;
   - questioning – plan some of the key questions you want to ask, some open, some closed;
   - target-setting – consider what targets you would like to see the teacher taking on, but remember not to force them.

Appraisal without the relationship – a sad case

With their preparations complete, both appraiser and teacher can face the interview feeling confident and assertive. Both have considered the performance of the past year, both believe they have identified its strengths and weaknesses and both know what they would like to achieve from the interview. If there has been a sound appraising relationship between teacher and appraiser throughout the year, this interview will be a natural climax to their professional work together. If there is not a background of co-operation and support, the meeting will seem strained and unnatural. In such circumstances the best the participants can hope for is that their meeting will be the foundation of an appraising relationship. Take the case of Walter Prickles.

Background

Pat Williams is the deputy head of Cwm Hapus school, a 1,000-pupil comprehensive, which prides itself on bringing out the best in pupils and staff. The headteacher allows the academic board to make many school policy decisions and sees it as the role of his senior staff to ensure that policy is carried out. Pat Williams has been at the school for six months. Walter Prickles, head of humanities faculty, has been there for five years. Pat is responsible for the work of the six heads of faculty and she runs their appraisals. The appraisal system began just before Pat arrived.

Tomorrow, having interviewed all other faculty heads, Pat will conduct a first appraisal interview with Walter Prickles. The headteacher believes that the first appraisal interviews with each faculty head are exceptionally important and is awaiting feedback on their success. The declared purpose of the Cwm Hapus appraisal and target-setting system is to evaluate performance fairly, to recognize achievement and to remedy shortcomings. Seen from their viewpoint, what kind of preparation will both participants have undertaken?

Walter Prickles' story

I'm Walter Prickles, a grade D head of humanities faculty at Cwm Hapus comprehensive. This year the school started an appraisal system and made me accountable to Pat Williams, the new deputy headteacher, who has six months' experience in the job. The head has decreed that the first appraisal and target-setting meetings are to take place this month, but I have been told by Pat Williams not to run my appraisals with the staff in my faculty until I have had mine with her. It seemed to me much more sensible to conduct my faculty appraisals first, but Pat seems to want to show me who's boss and so I've done it her way.

I'm 41 now, a geography graduate, and until a year ago I thought I was pretty much on course for a deputy headship. Not in this school; I don't believe in internal promotion to senior management. I don't believe wholeheartedly in integrated studies either, but was outvoted on the academic board and have tried to go along with that policy in the faculty. We have got as far as limited co-ordination, rather than integration as yet, of courses in years 1 and 2. Even this was not easy; each head of section is older than me and is opposed to integration. I find that much 'stick and carrot' are needed to keep the department going at all. I would like to see them motivating their own young staff, but I'm not prepared to step in and do that job for them.

My mother, who lives 40 miles away, has declined in health in recent years with a disease which has limited her mental capacity. Dad feels that she should go into a nursing home, but I have been supporting and encouraging him to persevere with helping her at home for a longer time. I have tried to keep this personal matter to myself and to my brother Geoffrey, a freelance writer, especially since he was largely coping with running the restaurant which mum and dad had previously run. The strain of helping Geoffrey at the restaurant and of supporting at home is beginning to tell on me and has led me to have the occasional day off, apparently with 'a severe cold'.

My former career plan and the proposed promotion now seem a long way away. For two years I virtually wrote the school timetable, ran the whole staff duty system and made the biggest school contribution to writing the school's TVEI extension submission. Now the worry at home, the change in school policies in which I get no guidance from the new deputy head and the complete absence of career planning, have led to a loss of interest on my part. Geoffrey keeps pressing me to join him in the restaurant business, but I would prefer, if possible, to get back my old enthusiasm. I love teaching and I still feel that with support and opportunity I could make it to deputy headship. Without this support I feel I could well give up teaching.

I have an appraisal meeting scheduled with Pat Williams tomorrow. I feel that she cannot criticize examination results or classroom performance which have been good. The few letters of complaint passed to me by Pat showed some slackness in marking homework, but otherwise could not be justified.

In the interview I would like

- To tell Pat how I feel about being 'instructed' not to hold appraisal interviews with my department. Couldn't we have had a meeting to discuss an action which, while it meant little to her, I found humiliating. At least we might agree a format for future communication.
- To explain how difficult I find it to press the introduction of integrated studies in the faculty. Could we set a realistic target concerning the extent and pace of its introduction? Maybe she has advice, techniques or support to offer which will make the management of the change much more successful than it is.
- To make Pat aware of my previous work at senior management level in the school, and at some appropriate time in the future have her welcome me back on to a programme of self-development and career planning.
- Tell Pat or the head about the reasons for what must look like sulking on my part at Pat's successful start in the school. If Pat created the right atmosphere I would explain the home pressure I am under. She might be understanding but I do want her to keep my family's problems private.

- Receive some credit, recognition and even praise for the quality of work in the department and its results.
- In short, I would like to use this appraisal to build an appraising relationship with Pat, so that in future, in our professional lives, we communicate more purposefully, frequently and easily.

Pat Williams' story

I am Pat Williams and I took up the deputy headship of Cwm Hapus six months ago. Full staff appraisal was introduced just before I arrived and I have the responsibility of managing and appraising the six faculty heads. I still have to be appraised later in the year by the head. All of my appraisal sessions are going well, but there is a problem interview ahead. The performance of Walter Prickles, head of humanities, leaves me with the feeling that he is increasingly allowing his staff to do whatever they will. Being a geography graduate, he has allowed the much older section heads of history, religious education and sociology to develop curricula which are clearly not integrated, even though the academic board agreed to integrate curricula in the lower school within faculties.

So that I could discuss this situation with him I sent Walter a note asking him to delay the appraisal interviews within his faculty until after our interview together. In any case, meetings are not a strong point of the faculty. Faculty meetings have never been frequent or dynamic since I have known of them; they seem to be held more to check minor administrative details than to be the powerhouse of discussion and change which they are in other faculties. Examination results are quite sound, but there is a hint that homework standards and marking are slipping, according to a few letters of complaint received. I allowed Walter to handle the complaints, since, to be fair, there are very few explicit examples of slackness. Yet, younger staff feel undeveloped, uninvolved and not stretched. I have tried to get Walter to spend time with these young staff but he is not interested.

Walter is only 41. He has been at the school for five years on grade D and, although an able person, he seems to have lost interest in work and promotion. Before my arrival, so colleagues tell me, he helped with timetable construction, duty lists and the TVEI extension submission. Now he works only school hours. I hope I have not put him off. He has been absent on 10 occasions this term, most of them for single days with 'a cold'. He does not seem to have personal problems. It is rumoured that he works in a restaurant run by his brother whenever he is away from school. He could be an asset to me and to the school if he could be as good as he is supposed to have been in the past. I feel that as a grade D head of faculty he should be setting a far better example. If he is not willing to set this example I am prepared to be firm and directive.

In the interview I would like

- To create a much better relationship between us. There is no appraising relationship comparable to those I have experienced in the past, nor to compare with those which are being built between the other heads of faculty and myself.
- To find out why his performance has deteriorated since about the time of my arrival, and offer the support the school owes him for his exceptional service in the past.
- To help with what appear to be real problems of a fossilized faculty staff at a time of rapid change in education.
- To discover if he wants to return to helping with senior management work. I could certainly use his experience and knowledge of the school.
- If all else fails, to tell him exactly what has to be done and make sure he does it.

There is no single format which will ensure the success of an interview, but in the interview between Walter and Pat we can identify some prerequisites. Most of Walter's hopes for a successful interview rest on his being given the opportunity to contribute and begin with 'tell', 'make aware', 'propose' or 'explain'. To encourage this Pat needs to

- Set a climate which encourages disclosure from Walter.
- Ask a balance of questions, beginning with such open questions as 'Tell me about your role in the school in the past', 'What problems do you see in the faculty?' or 'How do you feel our relationship could be improved?'
- Listen to Walter's replies. If the listener exhibits empathy Walter would like to discuss his dashed hopes of development and how family problems have affected his work.

Walter would also like feedback on his department. He could accept adverse comments if there was an acknowledgement of the good work being done there, too. Throughout the whole interview Pat should take every opportunity to reinforce the participative spirit; Walter would like to feel that he and Pat were working together on problems and this will benefit the long-term relationship with Pat. There must be consideration of Walter's current development needs. By meeting Walter's needs successfully, Pat will also achieve all she had hoped from the interview.

37
A MODEL FOR THE APPRAISAL INTERVIEW

This chapter provides a useful outline for appraisers to guide an appraisal interview.

Stage 1: Setting the climate

The climate for successful appraisal interviewing is relaxed, trusting and participative. Try to set this climate at the beginning of the meeting based on past relationships, but reinforce it whenever possible during the interview process. Climate creation is enhanced by

- Empathy. Glib claims that 'I know how you feel' from an appraiser who patently does not, can be annoying, but if an appraiser has had an similar experience and understands the teacher's position it will help to say so.
- Self-disclosure. Though the teacher does not want to spend the interview listening to the appraiser's reminiscences, it sometimes makes an interview seem less like an interrogation if the appraiser contributes illustrations from his or her own professional development.
- Support. Offers from the appraiser to support the teacher in appropriate ways remove the teacher's feeling that he or she is being judged rather than helped. It reminds the teacher that the appraisal process is about improving performance, not condemnation.

Stage 2: Opening the interview

Opening the meeting is another step in setting a participative climate. It consists of two techniques to start the meeting on the right lines:

1. Restating the purpose of the meeting. This reminds both appraiser and teacher that they have a task to accomplish together and suggests how they can go about it. For example, the appraiser might open with 'Well, John, the purpose of this meeting is for us both to look back at your work over the past year, then to plan the year ahead so that you continue to develop.' If an agenda has been previously agreed the appraiser can re-read it with 'We have arranged to look at . . .'. If the agenda is implicitly agreed to be total performance, the appraiser has the three appraisal documents around which to build the interview. The choice could be offered to the teacher, 'Would you like to begin by discussing the targets we set together last year, or with the basic task or with the awareness document which you have prepared?' At every stage the appraiser is reinforcing the participative theme which is the essence of successful appraisal.

2. Getting the teacher started. During an interview, the appraiser, having begun to introduce the meeting, often finds it difficult to pass the role of talker to the teacher. Have an open question ready which gives the teacher scope to carry the meeting forward: 'How do you feel about your first target?' or 'How do you see your performance of the basic task?' or, in fact, almost any of the questions from the performance awareness document which the teacher has prepared. These actions reinforce the principle that the teacher's perception matters.

Stage 3: Exploring performance

This stage of the interview can be seen in five sections.

1. Performance review

The initial step is to establish the facts about performance, both for the basic task – 'What were the GCSE mathematics results of 5C?' 'Were all reports handed in before the deadline date?' – and for any special targets set – the paper on assessment prepared for the governing body, running the Duke of Edinburgh Award scheme, rewriting the year 1 geography syllabus. It is difficult to develop an improvement plan if there is still disagreement over what has to be improved. Use the questioning techniques to give the interview another essential dimension by exploring the teacher's viewpoint in detail. Paraphrase and clarify to ensure understanding and summarize strengths and shortcomings to simplify the target-setting stage which comes later. Celebrate successes.

2. Performance analysis

Explore the reasons for the performance just agreed, especially the extremes of performance – the very good features and those which need improvement. Why were the science assessments so much better than expected? Can we create those conditions again? Why have relationships with the laboratory assistants deteriorated so badly this year? What has to be done to improve them? Celebrate successes as they appear or as they are analysed. See mistakes and failure as an opportunity to learn – a development opportunity.

3. Performance appraisal

Having established the achievements and the reasons for them, now is the time to agree an appraisal of performance. Now is also the time to agree the comments which will be officially recorded on each aspect of performance of the basic task and of targets. Where there is disagreement, refer back to the discussion and analysis stages. In my experience it is better to give the teacher the benefit of the doubt in writing these comments. Any weakness which the appraiser wanted to record but the teacher did not, will reappear in the course of the next few months, if the weakness remains, then both will recall their earlier discussion. It is more constructive to give time to agreeing the detail of the development plan than to spend time haggling over the precise phrasing of a weakness in performance.

4. Individual needs and aspirations

Much of this will come from the performance awareness document, for example courses needed, on-the-job training required, skills not being used, career aspirations, experience to be acquired. Encourage the teacher to be assertive. If the teacher will not say what he or she would like to happen, how are you, the appraiser, supposed to know?

5. Future job requirements

How will the job change over the next few years? How will the teacher have to change to be able to go on giving a good performance? Having become excellent in one style of teaching in order to achieve a particular set of targets, many teachers have found themselves stranded like beached whales when a new style is required for new purposes. Preparing to acquire those new skills early will increase confidence and reduce stress. It will also be a step forward in the achievement of the school strategic plan and in relating that to the personal development of the teacher.

Now we have all the information we need to be able to make development plans and set targets: weaknesses in performance, the teacher's aspirations and developmental needs and the planned changes in the job. Armed with this information we move to target-setting as our next stage.

Stage 4: Setting targets

Targets can be set to acquire or develop new skills, to set or maintain a standard of performance, to achieve a project or to implement a new policy. They can be individual, personal and professional targets, departmental and team targets or targets for the whole school organization. Whatever they are, the teacher has a right of input; he or she has the right to propose a target. The sections in this stage, therefore, are:

- Encourage the teacher to put forward his or her own proposals for target areas.
- Recognize the teacher's proposals and draw out others from what the teacher has said during your review of the year together.
- Discuss the merits and demerits of these proposals.
- Add your own suggestions, as appraiser, when the teacher is struggling to phrase a target in an agreed improvement area, or when you feel the teacher is missing an opportunity to develop.
- Agree a course of action, set agreed targets and record them, remembering to use all the target-setting guidelines:
  - description,
  - performance criteria,
  - measurement criteria,
  - priority,
  - feasibility.

Stage 5: Closing

- Briefly summarise in writing the key points of the appraisal discussion.
- Agree and sign this record, allowing each participant to add their own comments if they wish (see page 235).

Refer back in particular to one or two of the major accomplishments discussed earlier in the interview. Walk the teacher to the door, shake hands and return to the final part of the interview – the follow-up.

Stage 6: Follow-up

- Have a typed copy of the appraisal discussion and targets sent to those whom the system stipulates should receive one.
- Take any action which you, as appraiser, promised in the interview to take – course enquiries, meeting with other colleagues, planned observations, on-the-job training or interim review meetings.
- Review the success of the meeting for the quality of discussion, relationships, targets and motivation. As a result of the day-to-day relationship and the interview, the appraiser should have
  - reviewed performance and agreed on successes and improvement areas;
  - agreed on the factors which hinder performance;
  - improved relationships and mutual understanding;
  - clarified any uncertainties;
  - been made aware of the teacher's views and career plans;
  - defined new targets with the teacher;
  - agreed training and development plans.

Pro-forma for an appraisal statement

Part A. record of the discussion of the appraisal interview

1. The statement

A record of the main points of the interview, prepared by the appraiser in consultation with the teacher, including any conclusions reached. Be sure to include on this statement the positive features of the teacher's performance which have been identified. There are few enough occasions to include credit for good performance in appraisal documentation.

2. Individual comments

(a) Teacher's own comments ....

(b) Appraiser's own comments ....

3. Statement of satisfaction with the statement.

I agree that I am content with the above statement as a record of the appraisal.

Signed   Signed

Teacher   Appraiser

Date   Date

Part B targets for action

Target description

Completion date

Priority against other targets

Performance criteria

Results achieved

38
APPRAISAL INTERVIEW
PROBLEMS

Note-taking

Consultants in appraisal training are frequently told by appraisers of their concern with aspects of the interview. The most commonly asked questions are the following:

'Is it off-putting to the teacher if I make notes during the interview?'

Yes, it is if you make them surreptitiously. But if notes are made openly they enhance the importance of what the teacher is saying. If, when a teacher says 'I know I have run the department in your absence several times, but I have had no leadership training whatsoever,' you reply, 'It may be possible to arrange for some for you. It is important that I make a note of that' and then proceed to make that note, then it has a positive not a negative effect on the interview.

It is also wise to make the note so openly that the teacher can see it being made. This is especially so when beginning to frame a target. Many an experienced appraiser has passed the pen and paper to the teacher, saying 'Here, Brian, you phrase this target in a way that you are happy with'. In this case the record is being written so openly that either party can write it. If we are trying to convince teachers that appraisal is an open process, covert note-taking will hinder that process while overt recording will help it.

Timing the problem issues

'Isn't it best to bring up matters of concern to the appraiser early in the meeting?'

No. The danger with beginning the interview with these matters of concern is that your feedback on the negative aspects of performance is likely to determine the tone of the whole interview. I recall a Liverpool head giving feedback to a colleague who, he had previously told me was a great asset to the school and was giving a 95 per cent perfect performance, by saying 'Now sit down there Keith I want to tell you what your biggest problems are'. They never got off the topic. Keith had been expecting praise for his dynamic work during the year, with possibly some support for the few areas he still had not had time to develop. Instead, the whole interview was filled with criticism and eventually with bitterness and rancour. The head's strategy had been to get the criticism out of the way and then spend most of the remaining time in celebrating Keith's success. In practice, that did not work out. When, towards the end of the interview, the head did get in a word or two of praise it sounded to Keith like a sop to save a deteriorating interview.

Give the praise early, then people feel more inclined to be self-critical and are motivated to improve. Try to develop self-criticism through sensitive questioning. 'Which aspect of your performance are you least happy about?' 'Why is that?' 'What do you suggest we could do about it?' Such a series of questions is much more likely to be effective than the 'Here comes the bad news' strategy. Aim to make the balance of praise and problem-solving in the interview more closely reflect the teacher's performance.

Indiscreet disclosure

'What do I do if the teacher discloses more of his or her personal life than I need to know, such as revealing that there are marital difficulties at home or disclosing an "affair"?'

Sometimes the intimate nature of a one-to-one appraisal meeting does give the teacher an opportunity to unburden a personal problem. What could be the appraiser's response? Tell the teacher to keep personal life and work separate? Ignore the information and go on with the business of the meeting? Try a platitude or two such as 'I'm sure it will all work out'? Each of these would be insensitive. The only course of action is to allow the teacher to talk in confidence using the counsellor's greatest skill, the ability to listen. Empathize with the teacher if you can, or in some way show that you appreciate how difficult the situation must be. Such disclosure may take only a little time and it may be appropriate to return to the appraisal interview in due course. If the disclosures dominate the session, maybe you need the advice of a professional counsellor and appraisal may have to wait for another occasion.

Blaming others

'What is the best way to treat the teacher who becomes defensive and blames others as soon as we start the discussion of a certain topic?'

Let us assume the 'certain topic' to be one of the targets set by the teacher for the past year. When you refer to it in the middle of the interview you say 'Now shall we look at your second target which was to devise a common marking policy for the department?' The teacher replies 'You can't blame me for that! They wouldn't co-operate! Whose side of the story are you going to believe?' Or possibly the teacher shows defensiveness in another way, by not wanting to talk about the target at all.

A sensible tactic is, first of all, to reflect back the feeling that you seem to have detected. If reflected back in a way which is seen to be a comment not an accusation, this may encourage the teacher to explain the defensiveness. Second, try phrasing the question in another way to show that you appreciate the difficulties, for example 'I know you have made some progress with the difficult task of devising a departmental marking policy. Would you like to identify the chief problems which remain?' Third, try to make it clear that you are not trying to blame anyone, but to clarify problems. If none of these strategies works, then reassure the defensive teacher that you want to help to identify problems and devise solutions. Perhaps you should wait a while before bringing up the matter again on an agreed new date.

Unprofessional feedback

'What do I do if the feedback I receive from an appraiser does not follow the rules of feedback which you describe?'

Feedback should be fair and delivered in a form which the teacher can accept. It should contain nothing which has not already been mentioned during the year – the 'no surprises' rule. The teacher is asking, therefore, what do I do if the feedback is unfair, unexpected or badly delivered? The teacher is implying that, because of lack of confidence, feeling angry or upset, he or she may be uncertain how to proceed. I suggest the teacher uses a version of this well-tried formula:

1. Calmly ask for clarification, so that you fully understand what is being said. You could be over-reacting to something which the appraiser did not say or intend.
2. Avoid arguing, denying, justifying or reacting to it in a way you might regret later. Remember, the feedback you are receiving is only a point of view, not a final judgement.
3. Distinguish between the content of the feedback and your reaction to it. There may be truth in what is being said but you may not like hearing it under these conditions
4. Say you would like not to talk about it now but to meet again when you have had time to think it over. Take the time you need to think about the feedback. Talk it over with someone if you feel this will help.
5. Make your own choice about what you intend to do with the feedback – accept, partly accept or reject.

At the next meeting

6. Follow the practice of 'scripting' in this way:
   a. Make your statement. Say what you feel about what was said. Was it true, partly true or untrue? Let's hear your viewpoint.
   b. Empathize. If you can understand why the appraiser might misinterpret you or speak to you in that way, then say so. Try to show that you can see things from the other person's point of view. This will encourage the appraiser to do likewise for your viewpoint.
   c. Assert. Say what you would like to happen now or what you would like done about it by you or by someone else.
   d. Reward. Explain that you will be able to operate better, personally or professionally, once this matter is resolved.

All teachers who are required to manage other teachers and to act as their appraisers need to acquire the essential interview skills and to employ them. Their effective use will benefit themselves, their teachers and, ultimately, their organization and its beneficiaries – the students.

39
APPRAISAL AND MERIT PAY

How to avoid the dangers of direct linkage

I have argued elsewhere (Trethowan, 1987) that there is little scope for performance appraisal linked to annual salary. However, additional flexible finance could be used in the interests of stimulating and rewarding top class performance and in the interests of staff development. It would therefore be inappropriate to rehearse the arguments already put forward against directly linking performance appraisal with salary, except to point out one of the chief arguments against it. In the appraising relationship, the principle of the teacher contributing his or her perception of performance includes a willingness to identify in it weaknesses which the appraiser has not been able to pick up. In a system which offers the teacher support, help and development, he or she will be happy to do this. But in a system where any adverse comment on the teacher's performance could also reduce his or her next year's salary, the teacher is likely to conceal, to deny or to defend any shortfall in performance. Participative performance appraisal becomes, instead, the pedagogical equivalent of the teacher being expected to search for a stick with which to be beaten!

An example of a direct linkage of pay with performance would be the withholding of pay increments from teachers who were found to be unsatisfactory following an appraisal interview. The equity of the system is clear: the school should not expect to increase the salary of a teacher who produces an unsatisfactory performance. The disadvantage of the scheme is that it is aimed at improving the performance of only those teachers whose present performance is bordering on the unsatisfactory. Most teachers who produce a satisfactory performance will be unaffected by the scheme. It also implies that the school is perfectly willing to have unsatisfactory teachers on its staff as long as it can pay them a slightly reduced rate. This concept of being able to strike a bargain whereby a teacher does less or produces a sub-standard performance so long as he or she is willing to accept a salary without increments, is an enervating one. A much more effective guideline is 'full salary or no salary', bearing in mind all that has been written above about poor performers. In general, poor performers must develop on the school's improvement programme or their services are no longer required.

Another example of how salary and performance might be linked in a more positive way, and in a way much more likely to inspire excellent performance, is the system of flexible finance within a school to reward those who accept large or particularly important targets which are well above the requirements of the basic task. Such projects develop both school and teacher and can be of value far beyond the temporary additional payment which they attract. The message conveyed to other teachers by such rewards is an energizing one – that this school values enterprise, diligence and the search for improvement.

Even so, not all teachers can be motivated through a system of additional rewards, partly because there will be insufficient rewards to attract them and partly because people do not all have the same motivational needs. In the continuum which represents the range of teacher performances, only those near the borderline of an unsatisfactory performance will be affected by the possible withdrawal of incremental payments. Only those at the other end of the continuum, seeking to develop themselves or their establishments, will seek targets large enough to warrant project payments. The performance of the vast majority of teachers will not be greatly affected by either scheme; they will draw their motivation from achievement, recognition, responsibility, challenging targets, interesting targets, development, growth, working towards a promotion or from a genuine desire to do their best for the students in their care. There is no substitute for an appraising relationship in a school's teacher management.

Designing incentive pay systems

There are, however, some general guidelines for those designing systems of incentive pay.

- Remember the importance of the basic task; set reasonable levels for the incentive proportion of the total compensation package.

- Recognize the demotivating aspects of your incentive scheme.
- Ensure that the school culture and value systems are reflected in the scheme.
- Ensure individual and team targets relate to the strategic priorities and objectives of the school.
- Design a scheme which will allow a flexible response.
- Agree on measurement criteria for targets and be willing to use quantitative and qualitative evidence to inform the judgement.
- Involve team leaders in the design; draw them into the problem of rewarding individual performance against team results.
- Be sure the scheme is equitable across departments. Consider performance pay for behind-the-scenes staff, perhaps through the recognition and nomination of colleagues.
- Remember the keys to high performance lie more in achievement, recognition, responsibility and growth than in additions to salary *per se*.
- Evaluate your scheme regularly. Is it producing the desired behaviour?

40
THE WIDER USE OF PERFORMANCE MANAGEMENT IN SCHOOLS

Performance management for everyone in the school

Performance management works for everyone in the school – teachers, technicians, support staff and clerical workers as well as the bursar, the school secretary and the caretaker. Exactly the same model which we have described for teacher performance management is, in the best schools, currently also being developed for student and pupil performance management. It consists of a positive working ethos deliberately created by the adults who work there and individual target-setting both in achieving the National Curriculum and in personal and social development. Pupils, as well as adults, can be effectively managed using a style appropriate to their individual maturity in each situation. Telling, selling, participating and delegation are all styles used by effective teachers in the appraising school. Pupil assertiveness is encouraged at the expense of passivity and aggression. Much of the teaching in the appraising school is coaching towards self-development in missing skills and abilities. Good tutors form an appraising relationship with their pupils, and progress is examined by informed, sensitive joint reviewing of achievements at record of achievement interview sessions.

It can be no accident that an effective strategy for the management of people works whatever the age, qualification and experience of those being managed. The strategy is as effective in companies, churches, regiments and hospitals, as it is in schools; it is effective whatever the purpose of the organization – to make a profit or save a soul, to kill or to cure, to learn or to teach.

'Get out of the way'

If I may paraphrase the approach of Peters and Austin (1985), I believe them to be telling us that the secrets of people management are:

- Give people something worth while to do.
- Train them to do it.
- Get out of the way.

Robert Townsend (1970), who cannot be paraphrased, says, 'Provide the climate and proper nourishment and let people grow themselves. They'll amaze you.' Between them these writers have pinpointed a performance strategy for teachers: identify a worthwhile task, create the right climate, make sure people have the skills, give them encouragement and then manage them in a style which aims to 'get out of the way' as soon as possible. Teaching is inherently worthwhile work and is only made to seem otherwise by the restrictions and limitations placed on the task and by the conditions in which it takes place. Get the climate right, provide the development opportunities, adopt a management style whose aim is to move to the delegating end of the spectrum. Aim to 'get out of the way' and 'let people grow' and neither appraisal nor the appraising relationship will be a problem. You will be working in an appraising school.

BIBLIOGRAPHY

Anthony, R. N. and Herzlinger, R. E. (1980) *Management Control in Nonprofit Organisations*, Irwin Dorsey Limited, Ontario.

Armstrong, M. (1986) *A Handbook of Management Techniques*, Guild Publishing, London.

Belbin, R. M. (1981) *Management Teams*, Heinemann, London.

Blake, R. R. and Mouton, J. S. (1964) *The Managerial Grid*, Gulf Publishing Company, Houston, Texas.

Blanchard, K. and Johnson, S. (1983) *The One Minute Manager*, Willow Books London.

DES (1990) *Developing School Management: the way forward*, HMSO, London.

Fidler, B. and Cooper, R. (eds.) (1987) *Staff Appraisal in Schools and Colleges*, Longman, Harlow.

Francis, D. (1987) *Unblocking Organizational Communication*, Gower, Aldershot.

Hall, V., Mackay, H. and Morgan, C. (1984) *A Handbook on Selecting Senior Staff for Schools*, Open University Press, Milton Keynes.

Hall, V., Mackay, H. and Morgan, C. (1986) *Headteachers at Work*, Open University Press, Milton Keynes.

Handy, C. B. (1976) *Understanding Organisations*, Penguin, Harmondsworth.

Handy, C. B. (1984) *Taken for Granted? Understanding Schools as Organizations*, Longman, Harlow.

Heirs, B. with Farrell, P. (1986) *The Professional Decision Thinker*, Sidgwick and Jackson, London.

Hersey, P. and Blanchard, K. (1982) *Management of Organisational Behaviour: Utilizing Human Resources*, Prentice Hall Inc., Englewood Cliffs, New Jersey.

Herzberg, F. (1966) *Work and the Nature of Man*, World Publishing, New York.

Hodgson, B. (1989) *Job Descriptions*, Industrial Society, London.

Jones, A. (1987) *Leadership for Tomorrow's Schools*, Basil Blackwell, Oxford.

Kepner, C. H. and Tregoe, B. B. (1965) *The Rational Manager*, Kepner-Tregoe Inc., Princeton, N.J.

Maslow, A. H. (1954) *Motivation and Personality*, Harper & Row, New York.

Mumford, A. (1980) *Making Experience Pay*, McGraw-Hill, Maidenhead.

Peters, T. and Austin, N. (1985) *A Passion for Excellence*, Guild Publishing, London.

Peters, T. and Waterman, R. H. (1982) *In Search of Excellence*, Harper & Row, New York.

Schein, E. H. (1985) *Organisational Culture and Leadership*, Jossey-Bass, San Francisco.

Singer, E. J. (1974) *Effective Management Coaching*, Institute of Personnel Management, London.

Townsend, R. (1970) *Up the Organisation*, Hodder & Stoughton, London.

Trethowan, D. M. (1981) The Missing Link: Managing the Head, *The Head*, November.

Trethowan, D. M. (1983a) *Delegation*, Industrial Society, London.

Trethowan, D. M. (1983b) *Target Setting*, Industrial Society, London.

Trethowan, D. M. (1984) 'I'm going to make this school the best', *Times Educational Supplement*, 13 January.

Trethowan, D. M. (1984) Hole at the top, *Times Educational Supplement*, 21 March.

Trethowan, D. M. (1985a) *Communication*, Industrial Society, London.

Trethowan, D. M. (1985b) *Teamwork*, Industrial Society, London.

Trethowan, D. M. (1985c) in R. Blatchford (ed.) *Managing the Secondary School*, Bell & Hyman, London.

Trethowan, D. M. (1986) in C. Day and R. Moore (eds.) *Staff Development in the Secondary School*, Croom Helm, London.

Trethowan, D. M. (1987) *Appraisal and Target Setting: A Handbook for Teacher Development*, Paul Chapman Publishing, London.

Trethowan, D. M. (1989a) in D. Warwick (ed.) *Linking Schools and Industry*, Basil Blackwell, Oxford.

Trethowan, D. M. (1989b) *Staff Selection*, Industrial Society, London.

Trethowan, D. M. (1989c) *Team Briefing*, Industrial Society, London.

Trethowan, D. M. with Smith, D. (1984) *Induction*, Industrial Society, London.

Warwick, D. (1984) *Motivation*, Industrial Society, London.

SUBJECT INDEX